# Selected Poems of Jay Wright

. ON SERIES OF CONTEMPORARY POETS

For other books in the series, see p. 198.

Copyright © 1987 by Jay Wright

Introduction and Afterword Copyright © 1987 by Princeton University Press
Published by Princeton University Press, 41 William Street,
Princeton, New Jersey 08540
In the United Kingdom: Princeton University Press, Guildford, Surrey

All Rights Reserved

Library of Congress Cataloging in Publication Data will be
found on the last printed page of this book

ISBN 0-691-06687-6 Cloth
ISBN 0-691-01435-3 Paperback

Publication of this book has been aided by a grant from
the Paul Mellon Fund of Princeton University Press

This book has been composed in Linotron Sabon

Clothbound editions of Princeton University Press books
are printed on acid-free paper, and binding materials are
chosen for strength and durability. Paperbacks, although satisfactory
for personal collections, are not usually suitable for library rebinding.

Printed in the United States of America by Princeton University Press
Princeton, New Jersey

DESIGNED BY LAURY A. EGAN

# Selected Poems of Jay Wright

EDITED WITH AN INTRODUCTION BY
ROBERT B. STEPTO · AFTERWORD BY
HAROLD BLOOM

PRINCETON UNIVERSITY PRESS
PRINCETON, NEW JERSEY

# CONTENTS

## FROM *DIMENSIONS OF HISTORY* (1976)



## FROM *THE DOUBLE INVENTION OF KOMO* (1980)

# INTRODUCTION

## By Robert B. Stepto

> A young man, hearing me read some of my poems, said that I seemed to be trying to weave together a lot of different things. My answer was that they are already woven, I'm just trying to uncover the weave.
>
> Jay Wright, in a 1984 interview.[1]

Ralph Ellison has often scolded American audiences for thinking in distressingly simple terms about the purchase Afro-Americans have on American life and culture. Much of his complaint has to do with the ghettoization of a people and culture—in "ghettos" as small as a teeming urban district or as large as "the South"—and with all the attendant images: broken homes, broken lives, broken spirit; culture without civilization; potency without power; work without vocation; life outside history. In countering these images, Ellison frequently relates anecdotes, tales, and personal reminiscences about American life in what were once the country's western territories—places like Kansas, Texas, Ellison's Oklahoma, and Jay Wright's New Mexico. Wright, a much younger writer with different "territorial" memories, nonetheless acknowledges Ellison's strategy and message, and has recently exhorted in print, "Listen to Ellison on black African-Americans' intellectual and technical capabilities, and on their desires to work, to live and to be in the world that surrounds them."[2] Wright knows something of these capabilities and desires, and of their ability to create "cumulative communities" in history; he is intimate with these forces partly because he has *been to* these communities (destinations are one's true originations),

[1] Charles H. Rowell, " 'The Unraveling of the Egg': An Interview with Jay Wright," *Callaloo* 6:3 (Fall 1983), 12. This *Callaloo* number is a special issue on Wright.

[2] Ibid.

but primarily because he can imagine them—and imagine, too, the "enhanced world" they collectively form.

This directs us to a theme in Wright's poetry, but more than that, it instructs us about his increasingly specific interpretation of the poet's vocation as artist and as historian. For Wright as for Ellison—and others, too, including William Carlos Williams—the weave of community, history, and space is "already woven," and it is the poet's task to "uncover the weave." But what distinguishes Wright from these authors, and from many of his contemporaries as well, is that the weave he seeks to unveil or possibly reenact is from a loom of much larger scale. Whereas Ellison pursues the weave of a pluralized vernacular America ("America" meaning the United States), and speaks continually of the "fate" of that national geography, Wright unveils the strands and textures of the various transatlantic traditions of culture and consciousness.

Over the years, Wright has become more explicitly attentive to the tangle of black traditions binding the Americas to West Africa. One is therefore tempted to argue that from the view of literary history the poem behind Wright's art is Robert Hayden's "Middle Passage." It is worth suggesting that Wright's poetic act unlocks a Hayden line such as "Shuttles in the rocking loom of history." But claims of this sort for Wright's art are too culturally provincial and based upon too narrow a notion of what may constitute a precursory text. Wright has been "energized," as he likes to say, by texts and discourses as various as Dante's *Commedia*, Willard Van Orman Quine's work in logic, Benjamin Banneker's letters to Thomas Jefferson, J. B. Danquah's *Akan Doctrine of God*, and the jazz discourses of Albert Ayler and John Coltrane. In his art Wright is perhaps most obviously for New World readers an heir or sibling of Banneker, Hayden, Wilson Harris, Alejo Carpentier, Eliot, Hart Crane, and Nicolás Guillén. But Augustine, Goethe, Rilke, and unnumbered, anonymous griots, singers, musicians, and the like also figure in his ancestral community. To argue, as Wright has argued, that poetic discourse is that which handles its facts with more disdain than that of, say, the mathematician or chronicler is to argue as well a rather specific definition of who the poets are or have been.[3] This suggests the sweep and shape, as well as the discipline and drive, of Wright's aesthetic eclecticism. It suggests as well why he is now gaining the audience he has long deserved: Wright invites us to roam the cultures of the transatlantic world, to speak and know many tongues, to partake of the rituals through which we may be initiated into modes of individual and communal enhancement. In yet another age of great uncertainty, Wright enables us to imagine that breaking the vessels of the past is more an act of uncovering than of sheer destruction, and that we need not necessarily choose between an intellectual and a spiritual life, for both can still be had.

In risking a speculation about what Jay Wright has gained from being Afro-American and bicultural as a result of growing up in the American West (New Mexico, California), I hardly wish to suggest that he is some subtle, post-modernist sort of regional poet. Jay Wright is old Mexico and New Mexico; he is New York, New Hampshire, New World, New Modern. Perhaps New Jersey should be mentioned as well, since Wright pursued graduate work in comparative literature at Rutgers in the 1960s, where he was among the gifted as well as iconoclastic students of Francis Fergusson, to whom Wright dedicated his 1976 volume of poems, *Dimensions of History*. But in those days he was primarily of New York: an uptown man of letters in touch with the Village, working, as artists do, while studying, absorbing music while writing verse. In 1967, at the behest of Carolyn Kizer and with the help of Diane DiPrima, Wright published what he now prefers to call a "pamphlet" of poems, *Death as History*. Some of those earliest poems were soon more properly situated in Wright's first book, *The Homecoming Singer* (1971). Several of those, including "Crispus Attucks," "The End of an Ethnic Dream," and "Chapultepec Castle," appear in this volume as well.

The fact that *The Homecoming Singer* was published by Ted

[3] Ibid., p. 4.

Wilentz's Corinth Press is historically significant, for it allows a contextualizing of Wright within a particular group of young American "avant-garde" poets of the 1960s, poets who did not necessarily share the same poetic mission or idea of craft, but who were loosely a group nonetheless partly because they were Corinth authors. The list also includes John Ashbery, Diane DiPrima, Edward Dorn, Allen Ginsberg, Leroi Jones, Jack Kerouac, Clarence Major, Frank O'Hara, Charles Olson, Gary Snyder, Diane Wakoski, Anne Waldman, Philip Whalen, Al Young, and Louis Zukofsky.

What happened After Corinth is more a matter of which poet's career you choose to follow than of an aggregated, common fate. Ginsberg mellowed; Jones became Amiri Baraka, the protean poet and ideologue. Others in the luminous Corinth clan—Kerouac, O'Hara, among them—died; others still, including the Afro-Americans Major, Young, and Wright, struggle on with occasional teaching jobs and recognition, but pleased certainly by the attention certain presses now give to their talent.

In Jay Wright's case, four volumes of poetry have appeared since his Corinth debut: *Soothsayers and Omens* (Seven Woods Press, 1976), *Explications / Interpretations* (Callaloo Poetry Series, University of Kentucky, 1984), *Dimensions of History* (Kayak Press, 1976), and *The Double Invention of Komo* (University of Texas Press, 1980). This list informs us that the poet "uncovered" in *The Homecoming Singer*—"An aching prodigal, / who would make miracles / to understand the simple given"—has persisted in his search for that truth, and that he was especially prodigious at this work in the early 1970s. One observes as well that despite this energy, purpose, and production, and despite the award in those years of fellowships including the Guggenheim and the Ingram Merrill, Wright's work was published by very small presses—Kayak, for example. In the 1980s, the second and fifth pieces of what Wright has called his poetry's "comprehensive pattern" were printed by the new, university-affiliated Callaloo and Texas poetry series—the former an Afro-Americanist project, the latter more eclectically American as evidenced by its embrace of newcomer poet Vicki Hearne and former Corinth author Gilbert Sorrentino as well as Wright.

Callaloo and Texas have unquestionably brought Wright to new readers while bringing forth the missing volumes of the pattern. But publication is rarely also an act of clarification, that being one of the things a volume of selected poems hopes to achieve. A case in point here is the manner in which Wright's books are listed above: The publication dates are achronological, but the list correctly orders the volumes in terms of when they were composed and how Wright prefers that they be read. In a recent interview, Wright explains, "I have been following a dramatic movement, which the end of my first book [*The Homecoming Singer*] suggested and the subsequent books have challenged me to accomplish."[4] This volume of selected poems seeks to demonstrate that dramatic movement, and to suggest in the process that while it took Wright some fourteen years to publish the poems in the movement, what we witness in the series seen whole is a remarkable poetic sequence that was in truth the work of a magnificently productive decade.

Among Wright's readership, I detect at least three broad approaches to his art, based on certain poetic traditions. John Hollander, for example, remarks that Wright is "influenced deeply by Hart Crane, by Rilke and Hölderlin," and this provides him with the energy and vision to "not embark on any popular sort of quest for identity" involving the adoption of "the standard literary gestures (rage, irony, pity, 'doing the American voices')."[5] None of Wright's Afro-American precursors appears in this calculation, however, although Wright has acknowledged his debt to several "strict black brothers," including Banneker, W.E.B. DuBois, and Hayden. Hence, Wright has an Afro-Americanist readership in addition to the Euro-Americanist one; a readership that has occasionally

[4] Ibid., p. 13.

[5] John Hollander, "Tremors of Exactitude," *Times Literary Supplement*, 30 January 1981.

overemphasized the "black connection" much as the other group has the "white," but which justly contends that Wright's art draws as much from Hayden's reconfiguration of Crane's bridge—the rocking loom of middle passage—as it does from Crane's prototrope.

The third approach might be called revisionary comparativist; revisionary precisely because it knows that the predominating, Europhilic equations of comparative art and culture cannot fully calculate the figures of Wright's poetry. From this vantage point Wright's comment—"For my theoretical self, I have the examples and help of people like [Wole] Soyinka, Wilson Harris, and Robert Hayden"[6]—suggests a triangulation of transatlantic cultures in Wright's poems, which takes measure of this figure's scale and mass. Among Wright's professional readers, Vera Kutzinski, Cyrus Cassells, and Nathaniel Mackey seem to read him this way.

There are yet other nuances to the various receptions of Wright. Poet and critic Gerald Barrax insists, for example, that Wright is a religious poet whose "questing, eclectic, dialectical" verse is to be likened to the religious poetry of Yeats and Whitman.[7] Vera Kutzinski, who has written more than anyone else on Wright, stresses Wright's self-configuration as a New World poet who joins William Carlos Williams, Nicolás Guillén, Wilson Harris, and Alejo Carpentier in the task of discovering American history from a cross-cultural perspective.[8] John Hollander has addressed the claim that Wright is a myth-and-ritual poet and concluded, "Wright has long passed beyond the simplicity—however forceful—of merely asking what West Africa can mean for a bookish, learned, vigorously independent American poet."[9] With religion, history, myth, and ritual all in mind, I have studied Wright as a poet of per-

[6] Rowell, "Unraveling," p. 10.

[7] Gerald Barrax, "The Early Poetry of Jay Wright," *Callaloo* 6:3 (Fall 1983), 85.

[8] Vera M. Kutzinski, *Against the American Grain: Myth and History in William Carlos Williams, Jay Wright, and Nicolás Guillén* (Baltimore: Johns Hopkins University Press, 1987).

[9] Hollander, "Tremors."

formance and suggested, "Wright's art is one which forces us to make the all important distinctions between poems which describe or simulate performative acts—consider, among North Afro-American forms, the sermonic poem and the blues poem—and those which *prepare* us for performative acts,"[10] his poems being for me of the latter category.

Wright has many passionate adherents among his various readerships, as should any deeply respected poet. His poetry continually achieves its double goal of uncovering the weave of "the multicultural process of human history" while creating a collected readership that is in some measure comparably multicultural and hence, in Wright's terms, "enhanced." Aesthetically and socially, we gain from Wright's poems and from what he has thus far articulated of his poetics. Wright defines poetry as "a concentrated, polysemous, literary act which undertakes the discovery, explication, interpretation, exploration, and transformation of experience." He adds that he considers "poetry to have a functional value equivalent to all other forms of speech in a social and historical community." For Wright, poetry and the poet alike thus have "social and historical responsibilities," which leads him further to claim that "An unconscious artist is a contradiction in terms."[11]

Readers, like poems and poets, have social and historical responsibilities as well. Wright's poems awaken us to a most particular consciousness, one in which the full historical and human dimensions of a seemingly diminished world are arrestingly laid bare. As readers of Wright, we have the nearly singular opportunity of becoming one with what Wright so sparely calls our social context. This is so not because his poems are conventionally social, but because they are artfully filled with "desire's design" and "vision's resonance."[12]

[10] Robert B. Stepto, " 'The Aching Prodigal': Jay Wright's Dutiful Poet," *Callaloo* 6:3 (Fall 1983), 81.

[11] Rowell, "Unraveling," pp. 4-6, 14.

[12] From Jay Wright, "Desire's Design, Vision's Resonance: Black Poetry's Ritual and Historical Voice," *Callaloo* 10:1 (Winter 1987), 13–28.

# ACKNOWLEDGMENTS

The poems in this selection previously appeared in the following books by Jay Wright (listed in the order written): *Death as History* (New York: Poets Press, 1967); *The Homecoming Singer* (New York: Corinth, 1971); *Soothsayers and Omens* (New York: Seven Woods Press, 1976); *Explications / Interpretations* (Lexington, Ky.: Callaloo Poetry Series, 1984); *Dimensions of History* (Santa Cruz, Calif.: Kayak, 1976); *The Double Invention of Komo* (Austin, Tex.: University of Texas Press, 1980).

The editor gratefully acknowledges the kind assistance of Robert E. Brown, literary editor at the Princeton University Press. Equally invaluable was the advice of John Hollander, Harold Bloom, Vera Kutzinski, and Jay and Lois Wright.

## FROM

## *THE HOMECOMING SINGER*

## (1971)

## WEDNESDAY NIGHT PRAYER MEETING

On Wednesday night,
the church still opens at seven,
and the boys and girls have to come in
from their flirting games of tag,
with the prayers they've memorized,
the hymns they have to start.
Some will even go down front,
with funky bibles,
to read verses from Luke,
where Jesus triumphs, or Revelations,
where we all come to no good end.
Outside, the pagan kids
scramble in the darkness,
kissing each other with a sly humility,
or urinating boldly against the trees.
The older people linger
in the freshly lit night,
not in a hurry to enter,
having been in the battle of voices
far too long, knowing that the night
will stretch and end only
when some new voice rises
in ecstasy, or deceit, only
when some arrogant youth
comes cringing down front,
screaming about sin, begging
the indifferent faced women
for a hand, for a touch,
for a kiss, for help,
for forgiveness, for being young
and untouched by the grace
of pain, innocent of the insoluble

mysteries of being black
and sinned against, black
and sinning in the compliant cities.
What do the young know
about some corpulent theologian,
sitting under his lamp,
his clammy face wet,
his stomach trying to give up
the taste of a moderate wine,
kissing God away with a labored
toss of his pen?
How would these small black singers
know which Jesus is riding
there over the pulpit,
in the folds of the banner
left over from Sunday,
where the winners were the ones
who came, who dropped their nickels
into the felted platters with a flourish?
And how can they be expected
to remember the cadences
that will come again,
the same heart-rending release
of the same pain, as the clock turns
toward the certainty
of melancholic afternoons,
roast and left-over prayers,
the dampened hours that last through the night?
But Christ will come,
feeling injured, having gone
where beds were busy without him,
having seen pimps cane their number running boys,
the televisions flicker over heaped up bodies,
having heard some disheveled man
shout down an empty street, where women
slither in plastic boots, toward light,
their eyes dilated and empty;

will come like a tired workman
and sit on a creaky bench,
in hope, in fear, wanting to be pleased again,
so anxious that his hands move,
his head tilts for any lost accent.
He seems to be home,
where he's always been.
His intense smile is fixed
to the rhythm of hands,
to the unhurried intensity
of this improvised singing.
He seems not to know
the danger of being here,
among these lonely singers,
in the middle of the war
of spirits who will not wait for him,
who cannot take his intense glare
to heart anymore, who cannot justify
the Wednesday nights given up
in these stuffy, tilted rooms,
while the work piles up for Thursday,
and the dogs mope around empty garbage pails,
and the swingers swing into the night
with a different ecstasy.
Caught in this unlovely music,
he spills to the floor.
The sisters circle him,
and their hands leap from bone to bone,
as if their touch would change him,
would make him see
the crooked lights like stars.
The bible-reading boy tags him with verses,
and he writhes like a boy
giving up stolen kisses,
the free play of his hand on his own body,
the unholy clarity of his worldly speech.
He writhes as if he would be black,

on Wednesday, under the uncompromising
need of old black men and women,
who know that pain is what
you carry in the mind,
in the solemn memory of small triumphs,
that you get, here,
as the master of your pain.
He stands up to sing,
but a young girl,
getting up from the mourner's bench,
tosses her head in a wail.
The women rise,
the men collect the banners
and the boys drop their eyes,
listening to the unearthly wind
whisper to the peeping-tom trees.
This is the end of the night,
and he has not come there yet,
has not made it into the stillness
of himself, or the flagrant uncertainty
of all these other singers.
They have taken his strangeness,
and given it back, the way a lover
will return the rings and letters
of a lover that hurts him.
They have closed their night
with what certainty they could,
unwilling to change their freedom for a god.

# CRISPUS ATTUCKS

When we speak
of those musket-draped
and manqué Englishmen;
that cloistered country;
all those common people,
dotting the potted stoves,
hating the king,
shifting uneasily under
the sharp sails
of the unwelcome boats,
sometimes we forget you.
Who asked you
for that impulsive miracle?
I form it now,
with my own motives.
The flag dipping in your hands,
your crafted boots
hammering up the unclaimed streets,
all that was in that unformed moment.
But it wasn't the feel of those things,
nor the burden of the American character;
it was somehow the sense
of an unencumbered escape,
the breaking of a Protestant host,
the ambiguous, detached
judgment of yourself.
Now, we think of you,
when, through the sibilant streets,
another season drums
your intense, communal daring.

# THE END OF AN ETHNIC DREAM

Cigarettes in my mouth
to puncture blisters in my brain.
My bass a fine piece of furniture.
My fingers soft, too soft to rattle
rafters in second-rate halls.
The harmonies I could never learn
stick in Ayler's screams.
An African chant chokes us. My image shot.

If you look off over the Hudson,
the dark cooperatives spit at the dinghies
floating up the night.

            A young boy pisses
on lovers rolling against each other
under a trackless el.

      This could have been my town,
with light strings that could stand a tempo.

            Now,
            it's the end
            of an ethnic dream.

I've grown intellectual,
go on accumulating furniture and books,
damning literature, writing "for myself,"
calculating the possibilities that someone
will love me, or sleep with me.
Eighteen-year-old girls come back from the Southern
leers and make me cry.

Here, there are
coffee shops, bars,
natural tonsorial parlors,
plays, streets,
pamphlets, days, sun,
heat, love, anger,
politics, days, and sun.

Here, we shoot off
every day to new horizons,
coffee shops, bars,
natural tonsorial parlors,
plays, streets,
pamphlets, days, sun,
heat, love, anger,
politics, days, and sun.

It is the end of an ethnic dream.
My bass a fine piece of furniture.
My brain blistered.

# A NON-BIRTHDAY POEM FOR MY FATHER

Fathers never fit in poems,
and poems never please fathers.
On my father's seventieth birthday,
I tried to work him up a sonnet.
I guess I did,
and sent it off
with some kind of professional pride.
Everything seemed right.
He was seventy,
born October 25, 1896,
the numbers seemed to fit
in the proper mythological pattern.
I had my ritualistic materials,
his life, my art. Nothing could fail.
But he, with good reason,
never read my poem,
and I think he must have sat
in his small living room,
with the dying dog lying at his feet,
drowsing under the television's hum,
thinking how little I knew.
What metaphor was right
for the young boy,
fair and gray-eyed, with straight hair,
standing in the dry New Mexican evening
as his sisters offered him
the opportunity that they, black,
could never have?
Would he go off to medical school,
with Edmund Clapp shoes
and a Stetson hat,
court the high yellow princesses,

who drooled for doctors,
in a fifty dollar overcoat
and a blue serge box-back suit,
a diamond stick pin gleaming
against his shroud-like white shirt?
Not my father.
The trains would roll by at night,
the trucks would scatter cactus thorns
in their haste, big-muscled men
would knock down rocks,
and shoot a skyscraper straight to God.
Action was the tongue licking at that desert.
So he went away,
leaving his sisters to their perpetual blackness,
to find his own, or discard it,
to find his life in lines not yet laid out.
And things went fast.
A circus gig. Life in the hyped-up
masculinity of lumber camps.
He learned to drive a tractor on a boast.
And then into the New Mexico hills,
making red-eye that the feds
wouldn't bust because it always
got them there, and was clean, and safe.
Drinking and rolling drunk in the snow
with heavy women who could be Indian,
or at least, bragged that they were.
Having one son by a woman who had nine,
and leaving them both,
not really deserting them,
but not really knowing what to do
with either one of them.
And waking in the hills,
in a flurry, drunk again,
the salt used for a hangover cure
running into his eyes.
He had never seen a god,

and though he prayed at night,
whispering in his dark cabin
as he lay on the monkish cot
with his last cigarette,
he wouldn't spit near a church.
But that night he wanted
a vision and a promise,
and he got them—his own.
Out of the hills, off the juice,
straight to California and the money,
singing hillbilly songs on Central Avenue,
making love to the princesses,
who missed their doctors,
down by Wrigley Field,
taking the trolley out to San Pedro by the sea,
never to go back to the dusty black society
of New Mexico,
never to apologize to his black sisters,
lost, now, in their blackness and their dreams.
What metaphor can tell enough about the man,
stuck in credit unions, doing two shifts,
coming up with a taste for Dodges and diamond rings,
saluting with his very breath
the flags that disappear
on newly turned ships,
as they sink into the Pacific
oblivious of my father's faithfulness?
And there in the war hurried bungalows,
new friends came up out of the south,
and he took to them, their speech,
as if it were his.
He gave them his vision,
as they sat fingering old wounds.
His son would become a doctor,
grow out of this life
it took him such pain to make.
What would you say,

when all dreams lie so magnificently,
and sisters are moaning over the coffin
of some black princess,
dead a maid, dead in the dryness
of New Mexico, having caught a chill
in a flurry in the hills, looking
for that escaped prince,
who, once, as a boy, saw visions
of a life beyond their range?
The change was never in him,
but in the momentary bursts of black sisters,
pushing forward into what was everywhere
the gift of knowing the world,
as a seasoned bear will come from winter,
tapping through his unfamiliar home,
in spring, just as the light gives him eyes,
just as the small heat burns down
the way that salt will, in snow.
It is not a metaphor my father needs,
but a way of getting down
what it means to spring from the circle,
and come back again.
It is not a metaphor my father needs,
but a way of getting down
what it means to see his son run away,
in daylight,
run away into the crowded cities,
looking for that moment
in the dry and perfumed desert of New Mexico
when the father made his choice,
which the son must understand,
which the son must recreate
and see in the light of where he is,
where the father was,
and judge, not in innocence, but
standing at that point with his father,
getting down, without metaphor,

the years he cannot count,
the lives he cannot see again,
repenting the choices that sent
his black sisters, weeping,
to the grave of unwed princesses.

# THE HOMECOMING SINGER

The plane tilts in to Nashville,
coming over the green lights
like a toy train skipping past
the signals on a track.
The city is livid with lights,
as if the weight of all the people
shooting down her arteries
had inflamed them.
It's Friday night,
and people are home for the homecomings.
As I come into the terminal,
a young black man, in a vested gray suit,
paces in the florid Tennessee air,
breaks into a run like a halfback
in open field, going past the delirious faces,
past the poster of Molly Bee,
in her shiny chaps, her hips tilted forward
where the guns would be, her legs set,
as if she would run, as if she were
a cheerleader who doffs her guns
on Saturday afternoon and careens
down the sidelines after some broken field runner,
who carries it in, for now,
for all the state of Tennessee
with its nut smelling trees,
its stolid little stone walls
set out under thick blankets of leaves,
its crisp lights dangling on the porches
of homes that top the graveled driveways,
where people who cannot yodel or yell
putter in the grave October afternoons,
waiting for Saturday night and the lights
that spatter on Molly Bee's silver chaps.
I don't want to think of them,

or even of the broken field runner in the terminal,
still looking for his girl, his pocket
full of dates and parties, as I come
into this Friday night of homecomings
and hobble over the highway in a taxi
that has its radio tuned to country music.
I come up to the campus,
with a large wreath jutting up
under the elegant dormitories,
where one girl sits looking down at the shrieking cars,
as the lights go out, one by one, around her
and the laughter drifts off, rising, rising,
as if it would take flight away
from the livid arteries of Nashville.
Now, in sleep, I leave my brass-headed bed,
and see her enter with tall singers,
they in African shirts, she in a robe.
She sits, among them, as a golden lance
catches her, suddenly chubby, with soft lips
and unhurried eyes, quite still in the movement
around her, waiting, as the other voices fade,
as the movement stops, and starts to sing,
her voice moving up from its tart entrance
until it swings as freely
as an ecstatic dancer's foot,
rises and plays among the windows
as it would with angels and falls,
almost visible, to return to her,
and leave her shaking with the tears
I'm ashamed to release, and leave her
twisting there on that stool with my shame
for the livid arteries, the flat Saturdays,
the inhuman homecomings of Nashville.
I kneel before her. She strokes my hair,
as softly as she would a cat's head
and goes on singing, her voice shifting
and bringing up the Carolina calls,

the waterboy, the railroad cutter, the jailed,
the condemned, all that had been forgotten
on this night of homecomings, all
that had been misplaced in those livid arteries.
She finishes, and leaves,
her shy head tilted and wrinkled,
in the green-tinged lights of the still campus.
I close my eyes and listen,
as she goes out to sing this city home.

# W.E.B. DuBOIS AT HARVARD

In Harvard Square,
the designing locks
swing to your pace.
The bells push you
toward the teasing dons.
Bright boys begin to trill
their lamentable lessons.
It is too early for you.
All night, again, all night,
you've been at your
fledgling history,
passing through the old songs,
through the old laments.
But here, in Harvard Square,
the prosody of those dark voices
is your connection.
In any square,
the evening bell
may be your release.

# MORNING: LEAVING CALLE GIGANTES

The tart sun,
like a pink six o'clock grapefruit,
bursts over Guadalajara.
I have not slept,
have spent the night,
straggling with mariachis,
in and out of joints,
the extra instrument,
trying to sell my own song.
Now, I walk through streets
filled with women hump-backed with babies,
and move, pocketing my fists,
toward the bridge that leads to the market.
As I pass the clamorous church,
the perfumed candles drift and catch my clothes.
My own wet and beer-laden,
stale and anxious smell reaches me.
I see black-veiled women grovel
up the aisles on their knees,
their hands sweep as if they would clutch
and buffet me into penitence.
I stop, and wish for a guitar,
to send six light and deadly notes
riffling up through the nave.
Drunken and content, I move,
but am caught in a circle of little girls,
flying from the church like doves.
They do not speak,
but come with their small hands
folded piously near their pink chasubles.
Frightened, I walk as they,
as if we could not speak,

or walk upon anything solid,
almost as if we were plucked
from a garden to float in clear air,
silently spinning, as if the wind
would take us dancing over the traffic bridge,
past the market, until we would learn
to whisper, to beg to be released
and dropped where we would wither in good light.
I think that they could walk so forever,
unburdened by my smell,
waiting for me to speak,
or break the circle,
waiting, perhaps, for me to tear my shirt,
and scream, fall and roll stuttering
at their innocent feet,
rise and rip their innocent chasubles,
growl and gnaw at their innocent hands,
curse and drag them down on the bridge,
caught in their calm eyes.
They would not speak.
They have no language
to contain that kind of desire.
No Jesus can teach them
to flock like doves,
where I am waiting to stay my death
with theirs.

## CHAPULTEPEC CASTLE

This is the castle where they lived,
Maximilian and Carlotta,
and here is where Carlotta slept.
From the window, the city's streets
spread out like gray arrows,
lurching above the gardens in elegant
abandon. At this hour, it's true,
you can see the shiver of a forelock
off there miles in the distance.
In the winter, when the absence of leaves
mutes the summer's cellos, a shadow
stretches up to the headboard, where,
crutched in the drowsiness of dawn
and the emperor's distracted salute,
she would lie twiddling her able body,
slowly waking, listening
for any different drumming. Close your eyes.
The last echo of any movement
circles in the still room like cannons.
Not even the swing of seasons can blunt
that recognition. The subtle, historical
Mexicans, dying and hardly living,
were waiting, too. And Carlotta, tossing
in a fit of ancestry and half-conscious
dreams of a diaspora, must have thought
it marvelous to feel the gardens quiver to silence.

# AN INVITATION TO MADISON COUNTY

I ride through Queens,
out to International Airport,
on my way to Jackson, Tougaloo, Mississippi.
I take out a notebook,
write "my southern journal," and the date.
I write something,
but can't get down the apprehension,
the strangeness, the uncertainty
of zipping in over the Sunday streets,
with the bank clock flashing the weather
and time, as if it were a lighthouse
and the crab-like cars mistook it
for their own destination.
The air terminal looks
like a city walled in, waiting for war.
The arrivals go down to the basement,
recruits waking at five AM to check out their gear,
to be introduced to the business end of the camp.
Fifteen minutes in the city,
and nothing has happened.
No one has asked me to move over
for a small parade of pale women,
or called me nigger, or asked me where I'm from.
Sure only of my destination, I wait.

Now, we move out through the quiet city,
past clean brick supermarkets,
past clean brick houses with nameplates and bushy lawns,
past the sleepy-eyed travelers,
locked tightly in their cars.
No one speaks. The accent I've been
waiting to hear is still far off,

still only part of that apprehension
I had on the highway, in Queens.

The small campus springs up
out of the brown environment,
half-green, half-brown, covered over
with scaly white wooden houses.
It seems to be fighting this atmosphere,
fighting to bring some beauty
out of the dirt roads, the tense isolation of this place.
Out to Mama T's, where farmers, young instructors
and students scream for hamburgers and beer,
rub each other in the light of the jukebox,
and talk, and talk. I am still
not in Jackson, not in Mississippi,
still not off that highway in Queens,
nor totally out of Harlem, still
have not made it into this place,
where the tables creak, and the crickets
close up Sunday, just at evening,
and people are saying goodnight early.
Afraid now, I wonder how I'll get into it,
how I can make my hosts forget
these impatient gestures, the matching socks and tie.
I wonder how long I'll have to listen
to make them feel I listen, wonder
what I can say that will say,
"It's all right. I don't understand,
a thing. Let me meet you here, in your home.
Teach me what you know,
for I think I'm coming home."

Then I meet a teen-aged girl,
who knows that I can read.
I ride with her to Madison County,
up backroads that stretch
with half-fulfilled crops,

half-filled houses, half-satisfied
cows, and horses, and dogs.
She does all the talking,
challenging me to name the trees,
the plants, the cities in Mississippi, her dog.
We reach her house,
a shack dominated by an old stove,
with its smoky outline going up the wall
into the Mississippi air, mattresses tossed
around the table, where a small piece of cornbread
and a steaming plate of greens wait for her.
Her mother comes out, hands folded before her
like a madonna. She speaks to me,
moving step by step back into the house,
asking me to come again,
as if I were dismissed,
as if there were nothing more
that I could want from her, from Madison County,
no secret that I could ask her to repeat,
not even ask about the baby resting there on her belly,
nor if she ever knew anyone with my name
in Madison County, in Mississippi.

Since I can't, and will not, move,
she stays, with her head coming up,
finally, in a defiant smile.
She watches me sniff the greens,
look around at the bare trees
heaving up out of the bare ground.
She watches my surprise,
as I look at her manly nine-year-old,
drive a tractor through the fields.
I think of how she is preparing him
for death, how one day he'll pack
whatever clothes remain from the generations,
and go off down the road,
her champion, her soldier, her lovable boy,

her grief, into Jackson, and away,
past that lighthouse clock,
past the sleepy streets,
and come up screaming,
perhaps on the highway in Queens,
thinking that he'll find me,
the poet with matching socks and tie,
who will tell him all about the city,
who will drink with him in a bar
where lives are crackling, with the smell
of muddy-rooted bare trees, half-sick cows
and simmering greens still in his nose.

But I'm still not here,
still can't ask an easy question,
or comment on the boy, the bright girl,
the open fields, the smell of the greens;
can't even say, yes, I remember this,
or heard of it, or want to know it;
can't apologize for my clean pages,
or assert that I must change, after being here;
can't say that I'm after spirits in Mississippi,
that I've given up my apprehension
about pale and neatly dressed couples
speeding past the lighthouse clock,
silently going home to their own apprehensions;
can't say, yes, you're what I really came for,
you, your scaly hands, your proud, surreptitious
smile, your commanding glance at your son,
that's what I do not search, but discover.

I stand in Madison County,
where you buy your clothes, your bread,
your very life, from hardline politicians,
where the inessential cotton still comes up
as if it were king, and belonged to you,
where the only escape is down that road,

with your slim baggage, into war,
into some other town that smells the same,
into a relative's crowded house
in some uncertain city, into the arms
of poets, who would be burned,
who would wake in the Mississippi rain,
listening for your apprehension,
standing at the window in different shadows,
finally able to say, "I don't understand.
But I would be taught your strength."

The father comes down the road,
among his harness bells and dust,
straight and even, slowly, as if each step
on that hard ground were precious.
He passes with a nod,
and stands at the door of his house,
making a final, brief inventory
all around and in it.
His wife goes in, comes out with a spoon,
hands it to you with a gracious little nod,
and says, "Such as . . ."

"Such as . . . ," as I heard
when my mother invited the preacher in,
or some old bum, who had fallen off
a box-car into our small town
and come looking for bread-crumbs,
a soup bowl of dish water beans,
a glass of tap water, served up
in a murky glass.
"Such as . . . ," as I heard
when I would walk across the tracks
into Bisbee, or Tucson, or El Paso, or Santa Fe,
bleeding behind the eyes,
cursing the slim-butted waitresses
who could be so polite.

"Such as . . . ," as I could even hear
in the girded ghettoes of New York.
"Such as . . . ," as I heard
when I was invited behind leaky doors,
into leaky rooms, for my loneliness,
for my hunger, for my blackness.
"Such as . . . ," as I hear
when people, who have only themselves to give,
offer you their meal.

# THE INVENTION OF A GARDEN

I'm looking out of the window,
from the second floor,
into a half-eaten patio,
where the bugs dance deliriously
and the flowers sniff at bits of life.
I touch my burned-out throat,
with an ache to thrust
my fingers to the bone,
run them through the wet
underpinnings of my skin,
in the thick blood, around
the craggèd vertebrae.
I have dreamed of armored insects,
taking flight through my stomach wall,
the fissured skin refusing to close,
or bleed, but gaping
like the gory lips of an oyster,
stout and inviting, clefts of flesh
rising like the taut membrane of a drum,
threatening to explode and spill
the pent-up desires I hide.
Two or three birds
invent a garden,
he said,
and I have made a bath
to warm the intrepid robins
that glitter where the sun
deserts the stones.
They come, and splash, matter-of-factly,
in the coral water, sand-driven
and lonely as sandpipers
at the crest of a wave.

Could I believe in the loneliness
of beaches, where sand crabs
duck camouflaged in holes,
and devitalized shrubs and shells
come up to capture the shore?
More, than in this garrisoned room,
where this pencil scratches
in the ruled-off lines,
making the only sound
that will contain the taut,
unopened drum that beats the dance
for bugs and garden-creating birds.

# PREPARING TO LEAVE HOME

Trying to come out of it,
I see you shutter the windows
and silently pack my bags.
Here, at midnight,
even the rain is hushed.

I am not ready to leave this place,
and turn toward the wall,
hoping that you will stop and whisper
that it has all been called off,
or that, strangely, I've returned
without incident,
without having you sit and shudder
for my passage.

Outside, I can see
the last café bring down its metal gate.
A man in a white hat
leads a girl over the cobblestones.
Only one light, at the taxi stand,
stands off the assault of bugs.
Only one driver leans on his numbered car.
Only he and I are awake now,
and I go with one bag,
to offer it to him,
to deliver myself of it,
to ride unburdened in scented air,
coffined in the drone of his car,
moving as if we would glide on water,
toward other lights,
where I would deliver up all tickets.

I see no other passenger.
I hear the dank sound of an empty carriage

coming toward us, on wheels
that jingle like horses' bells.

I still hold myself from that other sleep,
but cannot say, now,
what sleep I shall enter here.
My eyes still insist
that I have not left you here.
I try to come out of it,
waiting for your whisper
to send me again into sleep.
The melancholy bells repeat themselves.
I have not prepared.
I have gone too soon.

## ORIGINS

We've been here alone for days.
You hardly move.
You sit by the fire,
cradling your Bible
in the canopy of your lap.

Once, as I woke,
still a little hazy,
the play of the fire over the pages
made the letters fuse,
and I thought you held a baby,
dressed in brilliant black,
shrouded and coffined in bone white ribbons.
Your hands moved,
as if they caressed it,
limb by limb, bone by bone;
you seemed to learn its rhythm.
I would have called you from it,
but could not.
It is better, I thought,
for my mother to embrace my delusions
than to have her call again
the death and loss of all her daughters.

Now, we wait here as one,
knowing my father walks the hills
east of Albuquerque,
where I have seen him speak
to Navajo runners, standing
with their feathered legs and arms.
And now perhaps he stands
like a stolid old chief,
in a thunder of drums,
with his discontent eyes staring past

the dancers, up the hills,
and has sighted a wolf,
stalking, asking to be captured
and wrenched into the ceremony.

Ah, mother,
even here alone in the room with you,
how can we lament your daughters,
born or unborn, dead or lost,
when the triplet drums
take our feet along the pearl gray ground,
where we can stalk down some other beast
with weapons we have never used,
in a strange tongue,
coming up at the top of a hill,
contemptuous of crosses,
beast-tall and naked as memory?

## IDIOTIC AND POLITIC

Your letter reached me
in the darkness of my fever,
when all my dawns
were some corrupt play of shadows,
when I was pulsing with the banal discoveries
we come to with such idiotic exhilaration.
Your candidacy is a fear I never held,
but now I fear your timid power,
brushing against the locks of our diffidence.
I can't imagine you a ghetto Solon,
linked to a line of escape.
But there are more tyrannies than service.
Holding your last statement,
I see your flippant breast cocking its way
into the canons of a careful city,
certain now of the creed's flexibility,
taking the ordered gestures as some sign
of consent.

Remember this.
Those nights we lingered
over the boldness of a dime not spent,
it was you, passionate
in holding passion in the bridge of our lives,
slack-eyed from your peripatetic graces,
damning our people as a world of beggars.
I had no strength then,
only the sympathy to adopt your eyes
and the brash rhythm of a seer
too wise to riddle.
Now, we go our separate ways.
I, even wiser now, a seer,
living in cities I cannot love,

and you, no longer a part
of the idiocy you engendered.
How politic.
But how like you, to find your historic form so soon.

Here I sit in the stolid temper of my study,
fidgeting with the system of a myopic Frenchman,
trying to find my politic self.
But this perversion mocks the Florentine,
would have stung the Philosopher to mockery.
And you, now unphilosophical,
have made up your mind to cozen ethics.
Oh, if I could reason now,
and find some determinate responsibility
lurching in the caverns of my mind,
if I could turn toward some beatific kiss.
There is a season all men dream of,
the ague released, all meanness brought to virtue,
no solitary captains and no wars.
But I walk in a city,
where harmonies are only heroic deeds,
marvelous paradoxes to the life of man,
myths to scale your life upon.
Your letter leaves me here.
Celtic kings would have smoked the night at your death.
Trumpet-tongued Roland would forget the art of
hesitation.
You would have held assemblies enthralled,
menacing the care of wives.
And all like you have ended there
where none began, the idiotic wax
of personality shaped by a politic temper.
Let this rest, and count no vote of mine.
There is something indignant,
paradoxical, and too true,
in the static flux of a life.

# DESTINATION: ACCOMPLISHED

Six miles between
my stop and this.
A Mexican night, a bus,
to diminish the bleakness
of New York's errant summer.

Mexicans flip like marlins.
A terrier yaps cadence
to a rhumba at the corner.
An untenanted Indian shawl
beguiles the neighborhood.

Six miles
of a Jersey turnpike
were never like this
and yet

those six vacant leagues
narrow in my memory
to a frieze

of inexpressible beauty.

But time to stop now
for this solitary room
where left-over patches
of yesterday fasten them-
selves to my melancholy,
a big and open patio to watch
a drunken fog insinuate
itself into the distance.
Back to these history books,
to my stroking of these beautiful,
discarded masks I keep.

A simple weight of all I am,
or would be.

This necessary chaos follows me.
Something to put in place,
new categories for the soul
of those I want to keep.
What I needed was to be thrown
into this toneless school,
an arrogant rhythm to release
my buried style.

This journey will end
with a double entry,
bought by poems
to all my hidden loves.

I have covered
more than six miles
to uncover
my necessary gestures.

From city to city,
from tongue to tongue,
I move in settled style,
a journey of the soul,
accomplished once,
accomplished
with what is mine.

## THE REGENERATION

The wind, taut as piano wire,
peels me apart.
I go down, down through the evening,
standing somewhere between light and dark.
On this hill,
I hear a child's voice
grumble like a soldier's,
and feel the weight of some dead man on my back,
his fingers tightened around my throat,
his brief knees tucked at my waist.
The child, at the summit,
calls into the darkness,
"I charge you to bury him."
I go on, where the wooden monuments
fall like banderillas in the leathery ground.
No light. No bells.
The flame of a cigar coming toward me.
A black man, in dashiki and crown,
holds his mutilated fingers in my eyes.
He asks me to count.
I cannot speak.
He sends me on.
The dead man extends his arm
along the ridge. I follow it.
We come to a shabby cathedral,
where three candles dance
to the wind's soprano.
Twelve men are going up,
under the applauding bells,
the seventh speaking in tongues.
In the circular cemetery,
there is wine bubbling
like the dead seething of a volcano.
We turn, framed like a manic caravan of flesh,

and go back toward the knees of the hill.
Down, down and into it,
with the cavernous city doubling like a bull,
the head pushed into the navel.
The body is singing to me,
"This is the gift of living in the fire,
of being turned to righteousness,
of being melted into some other
to become what you are."
The taut wind goads me,
undulating in the half-light,
now egg-shaped, now a fleshless embryo.

Now is the time to give up
the death of it your own dead living
the life what will not sustain you.

I run, under the dead man's stutter,
through these hills,
with these shadows,
to the ankles of the hill
and a green grave, an open coffin,
the morning's sheer cloak.
The dead man drops me there.
The shadows kick clouds over the grave.
The sun, taking the dusty air for a bed,
copulates with the moon.

# FIRST PRINCIPLES

I see my father
standing in the half-moon
that the ancient lamp
throws on the street.
There's broken glass
scattered on the sidewalks
like sugared diamonds,
all around him.
He looks a little strange to me,
almost ecstatic, as he stands there,
with his left foot planted
unconsciously on somebody's
discarded and torn shirt.
I walk toward him,
breaking my pace,
trying to approach him
as if there were no reason
to be in a hurry,
as if all that could be said
had been said, here, tonight,
among these broken windows,
these iron bars that squeal like pigs
when they're twisted.
I walk toward him
as if I didn't expect him to argue,
as if he would nod to me
in some silent acknowledgment
of what had been said over the splinters
of these pampered doors.
And yet I cannot believe
that he is here,
even if he's only come
to pick up the pieces,
to make sure I'm alive.

I can imagine his coming
to identify me,
lifting the sheet with emphatic hands,
nodding briefly and turning out
into the crowd, where he could
bury himself and scream tears,
as if he were one of them,
giving in to his rage,
and not his loss.
Or I can imagine him,
going down white-washed halls,
in the groaning wards,
where men are hammering at their eyes,
as their sons tell them
what the streets were like,
try to describe the feel
of being bludgeoned half into death,
half into the silly exhilaration
of letting go of everything,
reaching out and whirling
toward the center of yourself
and feeling that, if you grasped it,
you would be caught there,
suspended like a leaf
bottled in the wind
with no place to drop.
But he is there.
And I'm alive, for the moment,
still the lively son of a man,
who is the lively son
of a railroad man,
who came up out of the south,
telling lies about his age,
his work, his place of birth,
his stolid wife, tricking everyone,
including himself,
so *that* moment would come

when he would see his son
move from being only a son
and change his own truth
to probable lies, going off
as if he were being born
at the foot of death.
And I'm walking, now,
prepared to argue with that man,
who has his foot on the tattered shirt.
I hear it coming from me like a text,
my biblical, righteous rhetoric:
how can I tell you
the absolute rightness
of being in this fire?
how could I turn back?
for this is certain,
and I can't sit, now,
on your darkened porch,
like a scholar,
telling you that when dancers
argue with the earth,
and black men speak in tribal tongues,
it is not a festival of the damned,
it is a feast of the living,
who move toward the past,
not in the fantastic,
but in the certainty of myth,
in the tongues of the exiled dead,
who live in the tongues of the living.
Walking here,
I still feel I can sing
like a poet, a mad prophet,
caught up in my own cadences,
while my father stands,
drawing in his breath,
prepared to run to me,
prepared to save me.

I look at him,
in the half-moon of the light.
He lifts his hand,
and I listen to him breathe
in the tongues of the exiled dead.

# SKETCH FOR AN AESTHETIC PROJECT

I believe now that love is half persistence,
A medium in which, from change to change,
Understanding may be gathered.

Thomas Kinsella / *Nightwalker*

1

I stomp about these rooms in an old overcoat,
never warm, but never very anxious
to trot off to the thickly banked park,
where the perpetual rain hangs in the trees,
even on sunny days.

When I step out,
the streets are cleaned of life,
only, perhaps,
an old woman in black,
staggering along with a lantern,
only, perhaps,
a burro decked out under a pair of straw baskets,
or a dim-eyed student
lingering at a grilled window, listening to whispers.
Just as in forgotten cities,
there is hardly a sound,
hardly a movement, or a light.
I clatter over cobbled streets,
listening, watching.
I pretend not to be afraid of witches,
or any forces,
ground down under the years here,
carping and praying under stones,
calling curses down on unthinking walkers,
who go, as I do, timid and fleet,
toward their own purposes.

I can only hope to meet some other soul,
tugging a burro up the street,
loaded with wet wood,
padding barefoot through the rain,
coming toward me, hard-mouthed,
holding his faintly gabled hands
to pluck my pity.

2

I call this home.
And like a traveler home from seeing,
I walk my flowered stairs,
and reconstruct my journeys,
remembering every brick and bird,
recalling the miracle of being there.
But names are what I call again.
New York. And call it home.
Again, I walk in summer, innocently,
a long walk, down Seventh, Harlem,
twisting and finding new turns.
The streets breathe again.
The lights scorch the midway islands.
Voices dance at the edges.
An abandoned store begins to howl
with camp meeting songs.
I am there again,
under the eyes of the man they call the deacon,
a rabbi of the unscrupulous.
His eyes are as taut and brilliant as marble.
He babbles about shoes and croaker sacks.
Old women flail at kids, and return to gossip.
They watch the rabbi pass.
They watch me pass.
Even here, I am there again.
And those succulent voices drive me mad.

3

Wake, and the lights bob like tongueless bells.
Churches spew catholic clad blessed ones.
I wait, here near the ocean, for the north wind,
and the waves breaking up on ships.
At this point, the slave ships would dock,
creeping up the shore-line,
with their bloody cargo intact,
the ingenuous sailors unnerved
through days of hopeless waiting,
hopeless anticipation of reward,
hopeless clutching at the dying,
then intensely buoyed by sight of land
and the fervent release of cankered bodies.
At this point, I wait,
and cannot go back to linger on my stairs,
or grovel under the deacon's eyes.
I have made a log for passage,
out there, where some still live,
and pluck my bones.
There are parchments of blood,
sunk where I cannot walk.
But when there is silence here,
I hear a mythic shriek.

4

This shriek in the coldness
is like music returning to me,
coming over the illusion of solitude,
swift and mad as I am,
dark in its act,
light
in the way it fills
my pitiless mind.

## BEGINNING AGAIN

1

I've come back so slowly,
to here, trying to remember
how I came here then,
what sense of speaking
brought me to this place.
My history is like a bird's,
flying away, nesting
wherever sun and some small
charity are offered to me,
pecking in rain and ill-fortune,
when they come, only to survive
as one whose virtue is flying.
But I am more than a bird,
and less, being weighted
and buoyed by a sense of tongues,
being kept in my voluntary flight
because I am impressed
with weight other than my own,
being sure that my routes are chosen,
sure that there is a changeless place
that holds me, that will not be shaken.

So leave the history of birds,
even their ash-scented flowering,
even their holy beauty.
I return to tell how
I come back so slowly,
carefully, to here,
where you see me now.

2

Ah, the pain I could tell,
but that is not my choice.

Before you, I'm not even virtuous.
Sulking and skulking in old bones,
I ravish cities, shredding rich cloth,
picking golden coins,
spading up shards of faded vessels
that tell me nothing.
I sit in semestral light
like Chekhov's old student
annotating manuscripts,
looking for something to oppose your arrogance.
But I write here, speaking to you,
where discoveries end,
opposed within myself,
but here now at the edge,
where something must speak
for us, to us, for me, alone.

3

The bridge is open.
The night of the bay falls
liberally to the water.
The lamps are lit past paling time.
I think of how
I walked this bridge,
and would have leaped,
leaving only my wallet
to identify me,
leaving without a scream,
splayed and sucked
by the eddying water,
my life the still center
of the ocean smoothing
its deadly wrinkles.
That is the history of a dream,
of one life choosing its end.
We cannot all choose so.
And at the foot of the bridge,

two lovers walk on the can burdened sand,
a portable radio fusing their twin heads,
their stripped shoes leaking garbage.
They are not lonely or lost.
They speak from the other side
of the bridge; they walk toward
a car, to drift toward a lighted house,
with the smell of meat
and unintended parties waiting there.

4

Ah, but I'vc come away
from that death desire.
Walking in soggy alleys,
my ears beaten by the cock
and preening crull of other tongues,
I haven't wanted that.
I will lay you a limbo
of soft afternoons,
with peacocked drinks
and street dances,
take you through the square
in Vera Cruz, where you can hear
your indiscretions sung by La Negra,
her bombastic harp nursing
your pesos in the womb of its bridge.
There, we turn away, and float,
while the three o'clock camphor
settles in the square, and La Negra
wobbles silently toward home,
her cuddled harp cradled
in one restless hand.

5

"Everything rhythmically organic is true."
La Negra's harp.

The voices I cannot claim.
Even the memory of a dead bird,
coming to rest in my life.
And now my ancient rhythm calls me,
out of ashes and fraternal death,
"Before you, mother Idoto,
naked I stand . . .
a prodigal . . .
lost in your legend . . ."
An aching prodigal,
who would make miracles
to understand the simple given.

# FROM

# *SOOTHSAYERS AND OMENS*

# (1976)

# BENJAMIN BANNEKER HELPS TO BUILD A CITY

In a morning coat,
hands locked behind your back,
you walk gravely along the lines in your head.
These others stand with you,
squinting the city into place,
yet cannot see what you see,
what you would see
—a vision of these paths,
laid out like a star,
or like a body,
the seed vibrating within itself,
breaking into the open,
dancing up to stop at the end of the universe.
I say your vision goes as far as this,
the egg of the world,
where everything remains, and moves,
holding what is most against it against itself,
moving as though it knew its end, against death.
In that order,
the smallest life, the small event take shape.
Yes, even here at this point,
Amma's plan consumes you,
the prefigured man, Nommo, the son of God.
I call you into this time,
back to that spot,
and read these prefigurations
into your mind,
and know it could not be strange to you
to stand in the dark and emptiness
of a city not your vision alone.

Now, I have searched the texts
and forms of cities that burned,

that decayed, or gave their children away,
have been picking at my skin,
watching my hand move,
feeling the weight and shuttle of my body,
listening with an ear as large as God's
to catch some familiar tone in my voice.
Now, I am here in your city,
trying to find that spot
where the vibration starts.
There must be some mistake.

Over the earth,
in an open space,
you and I step to the time
of another ceremony.
These people, changed,
but still ours,
shake another myth
from that egg.
Some will tell you
that beginnings are only
possible here,
that only the clamor of these drums
could bring our God to earth.
A city, like a life,
must be made in purity.

So they call you,
knowing you are intimate with stars,
to create this city, this body.
So they call you,
knowing you must purge the ground.

"Sir, suffer me to recall to your mind that time,
in which the arms and tyranny of the British crown
were exerted, with every powerful effort, in order

to reduce you to a state of servitude: look back,
I entreat you, on the variety of dangers to which
you were exposed; reflect on that time, in which
every human aid appeared unavailable, and in which
even hope and fortitude wore the aspect of inability
to the conflict, and you cannot but be led to a serious
and grateful sense of your miraculous and providential
preservation; you cannot but acknowledge, that the present
freedom and tranquility which you enjoy you have mercifully
received, and that it is the peculiar blessing of Heaven."

"Reflect on that time."
The spirits move, even
in the events of men,
hidden in a language
that cannot hide it.
You were never lost
in the language of number alone;
you were never lost
to the seed vibrating alone,
holding all contradictions within it.
"Look back, I entreat you,"
over your own painful escapes.

The seed now vibrates into a city,
and a man now walks where you walked.
Wind and rain must assault him,
and a man must build against them.
We know now, too, that the house
must take the form of a man
—warmth at his head, movement at his feet,
his needs and his shrine at his hands.
Image of shelter, image of man,
pulled back into himself,
into the seed before the movement,
into the silence before the sound

of movement, into stillness,
which may be self-regard,
or only stillness.

Recall number.
Recall your calculations,
your sight, at night,
into the secrets of stars.
But still you must exorcise this ground.

"Here was a time, in which your tender feelings
for yourselves had engaged you thus to declare,
you were then impressed with proper ideas of the
great violation of liberty, and the free possession
of those blessings, to which you were entitled by nature;
but, Sir, how pitiable it is to reflect, that although
you were so fully convinced of the Father of Mankind,
and of his equal and impartial distribution of these
rights and privileges, which he hath conferred upon
them, that you should at the same time counteract his
mercies, in detaining by fraud and violence so numerous
a part of my brethren, under groaning captivity,
and cruel oppression, that you should at the same time
be found guilty of that most criminal act, which you
professedly detested in others, with respect to yourselves."

Can we say now
that it is the god
who chains us to this place?
Is it this god
who requires the movement,
the absence of movement,
the prefiguration of movement
only under his control?
If so,
what then is the reason
for these dancers,

these invocations,
the sight of these lesser gods
lining out the land?
How pitiable it is to reflect
upon that god, without grace,
without the sense of that small
beginning movement,
where even the god
becomes another and not himself,
himself and not another.
So they must call you,
knowing you are intimate with stars;
so they must call you,
knowing different resolutions.
You sit in contemplation,
moving from line to line,
struggling for a city
free of that criminal act,
free of anything but the small,
imperceptible act, which itself becomes free.
Free. Free. How will the lines fall
into that configuration?
How will you clear this uneasiness,
posting your calculations and forecasts
into a world you yourself cannot enter?
Uneasy, at night,
you follow stars and lines to their limits,
sure of yourself, sure of the harmony
of everything, and yet you moan
for the lost harmony, the crack in the universe.
Your twin, I search it out,
and call you back;
your twin, I invoke
the descent of Nommo.

I say your vision goes as far as this.
And so you, Benjamin Banneker,

walk gravely along these lines,
the city a star, a body,
the seed vibrating within you,
and vibrating still,
beyond your power,
beyond mine.

# BENJAMIN BANNEKER SENDS HIS *ALMANAC* TO THOMAS JEFFERSON

Old now,
your eyes nearly blank
from plotting the light's
movement over the years,
you clean your *Almanac*,
and place it next
to the heart of this letter.
I have you in mind,
giving a final brush and twist
to the difficult pages,
staring down the shape of the numbers
as though you would find a flaw
in their forms.
Solid, these calculations
verify your body on God's earth.
At night,
the stars submit themselves
to the remembered way you turn them;
the moon gloats under your attention.
I, who know so little of stars,
whose only acquaintance with the moon
is to read a myth, or to listen
to the surge
of songs the women know,
sit in your marvelous reading
of all movement,
of all relations.

So you look into what we see
yet cannot see,

and shape and take a language
to give form to one or the other,
believing no form will escape,
no movement appear, nor stop,
without explanation,
believing no reason is only reason,
nor without reason.
I read all of this into your task,
all of this into the uneasy
reproof of your letter.

Surely, there must be a flaw.
These perfect calculations fall apart.
There are silences
that no perfect number can retrieve,
omissions no perfect line could catch.
How could a man but challenge God's
impartial distributions?
How could a man sit among
the free and ordered movements
of stars, and waters, beasts and birds,
each movement seen or accounted for,
and not know God jealous,
and not know that he himself must be?

So you go over the pages again,
looking for the one thing
that will not reveal itself,
judging what you have received,
what you have shaped,
believing it cannot be strange
to the man you address.
But you are strange to him
—your skin, your tongue,
the movement of your body,
even your mysterious ways with stars.
You argue here with the man and God,

and know that no man can be right,
and know that no God will argue right.
Your letter turns on what the man knows,
on what God, you think, would have us know.
All stars will forever move under your gaze,
truthfully, leading you from line to line,
from number to number, from truth to truth,
while the man will read your soul's desire,
searcher, searching yourself,
losing the relations.

# THE ALBUQUERQUE GRAVEYARD

It would be easier
to bury our dead
at the corner lot.
No need to wake
before sunrise,
take three buses,
walk two blocks,
search at the rear
of the cemetery,
to come upon the familiar names
with wilted flowers and patience.
But now I am here again.
After so many years
of coming here,
passing the sealed mausoleums,
the pretentious brooks and springs,
the white, sturdy limestone crosses,
the pattern of the place is clear to me.
I am going back
to the Black limbo,
an unwritten history
of our own tensions.
The dead lie here
in a hierarchy of small defeats.
I can almost see the leaders smile,
ashamed now of standing
at the head of those
who lie tangled
at the edge of the cemetery
still ready to curse and rage
as I do.
Here, I stop by the imitative cross

of one who stocked his parlor
with pictures of Robeson,
and would boom down the days,
dreaming of Othello's robes.
I say he never bothered me,
and forgive his frightened singing.
Here, I stop by the simple mound
of a woman who taught me
spelling on the sly,
parsing my tongue
to make me fit for her own dreams.
I could go on all day,
unhappily recognizing small heroes,
discontent with finding them here,
reproaches to my own failings.
Uneasy, I search the names
and simple mounds I call my own,
abruptly drop my wilted flowers,
and turn for home.

# FAMILY REUNION

Each time we meet,
you stare at my nose and eyes,
my cleft chin and high forehead,
and find an unfamiliar relative's traces.
And here you sit and thrust
the family photo album on me,
slip snapshots from the book,
clap them into my hand
the way you would a spoon in a baby's.

In a voice as high and lazy
as a mountain stream,
you enchant us with your own rewards.
Christian tales and triumphs leap from you.
I remember now the German drunk,
puking and sprawling down your ghetto alley,
lost, until he sailed into your house,
into your arms, into your pity
and his miraculous salvation.
Or you could tell us again
about the night you prayed all night,
having given your elders and saints
an ultimatum on the last request
your landlord made to you,
and woke the next morning to find
dollars as common as leaves on your table.

But why should I find this strange?
You have always had the gift
of looking in eyes,
and finding the touch of another there;
of stepping into the day's sun,
and being able to measure it
against every other;

of hearing a voice, and being able to coax
the speaker into echoes of himself, his selves,
his forgotten voices, voices he had never heard;
of calling your own name, and having it belled
back in tongues, being changed and harmonized
until it is one name and all names.

My saintly sister,
you are more than a woman,
more than the saintly body and soul
you desire for yourself.
You tell me,
but I know you do not walk
with Jesus or his saints,
nor do you grovel up the paths
you know he took.
You bless, save, rage
and turn yourself sinners from the temple.
Close to the book,
your eyes hint that I must be one of them.
Am I your final disgrace?
Is it the book alone itself
that has caught me moving away from you?
Among these images you know so well,
will you finally recognize me?

# BAPTISM IN THE LEAD AVENUE DITCH

Ageless again,
I stand on this bridge of railroad ties,
and hear the lion's purr of trains
pausing between Chicago and Los Angeles,
the swish of steam,
the water whipped over their heads
to beat away the unconsecrated dust
of the deserts they pass through.
In the evening,
the grain-brick patio hotel
is a cathedral.
Pigeons roost like doves.
Navajo stroll under the naves,
robed in rugs and special beads.
Bells, boasting in a nearby adobe church,
calm the streets.
All travelers are held in silence.
This is the stillness
from which the night will come.
This is the stillness
from which all travelers will set out.

At night, I climb
the lonely cypress on the ditch bank,
and see our neighbor and her daughter
steal down the street,
barefoot, erect and balancing
bundles on their heads.
I hold my breath,
and try not to shake my tree house,
so high away I only hear
the melancholy slap of their hands,

and see them move from side to side,
dressing the cypress in their wet clothes,
passing and coming so close to each other
that I cannot tell them apart,
cannot separate them when they part.
Sometimes, they sing or moan in a language
that, even knowing them,
I cannot understand.

Now, at twelve,
I rise in the singing to confess.
All morning,
every eye has been turned toward me,
the only one still unbaptized,
the only one who has never spoken,
the one who has kept the common light
in his own darkness,
sitting at the edge of the circle,
in shadows,
listening to the common life,
raveled, piece by piece,
into a story even I can tell.
I tell it now.
And now, at twelve,
I walk with the others,
along the ditch bank,
out where the hoot of the trains
comes like the weak howl of a wolf.
Robed in white,
I step into the preacher's arms.

The best time to arrive
is just at sunrise,
come, cushioned in a coach,
along the mountains turning gray,
reddening out into a golden bronze.
The pale green cacti

line the land like crosses,
breaking at the top with pink and white flowers.
Even the buzzards,
diving after cow carcasses,
circling the dark clouds,
caught in the halo of the still dying moon,
become beautiful.
I pass through this silence,
again and again,
down into a silent valley,
where the streets fill with Catholic bells,
and a donkey, loaded with pails,
moves from house to house.

You come into the stillness that remains,
at night,
and move in my river,
under my eyes,
and beat the shame from your clothes.
I lean down,
and see my image in the water,
and wonder, if I fell,
if you would robe me in a sheet
like a baptized boy,
or strip me and make me dance between you,
embracing one and then the other.
Was it here, at this point,
that I stepped into the preacher's arms?
Was it here, at this point,
that I caught the travelers' cathedral
moving into the darkness?
Night after night,
I take your voices and your bodies
back into my apprehension.
Mother and daughter,
night after night,
you beat my absence into the water.

Under this water,
all sounds come like thunder.
Familiar voices are lost.
God's man has his hand,
like a mask, over my face,
and still I suck up mud
and the taste of dry grass,
hear the deep tone of a bell
struck at the bottom of an ocean,
see fire chase down flashes of light,
feel my head swell.
I rise in pure water,
unashamed.
You see me,
and find me washed clean.

I lean down now,
and push the thick mud away,
to look for your footstep,
and think, with the first touch of rage,
that you may even be buried there.
I move, and return
to this city stripped of movement,
remembering that I entered its holiness,
by your side,
my fingers already filled with its death.

## NIGHT RIDE

A lame horse moves
along the edge of a stream.
You are on his unsaddled back,
leaning into the soft buttocks
of a girl. Your arms extend
over the girl's thighs,
down around the horse's neck.
It is that rainbow evening
that comes at times
at the end of a gentle rain,
or at the end of a day so fierce
the crickets slug through their songs,
casting a sorcerer's eye at anyone
who would choose to move.
We should not be out past dark,
but no one can tell
if it is the sun or the moon
swaying in the hammock of the sky.
Off in the distance, I hear
the old folks create a canon
out of June bugs and junipers,
a lemonade, sweet peaches,
an empty moon over an empty garden.
I would follow you
down the muddy back reaches of the stream,
and wait when the horse stops
to lift his lame leg
and drop his heavy, straw-scented load,
and wait when you stop
to caress the horse's neck,
or to reason out the moon.
It is an old path we take.
The ridges rise with familiar bumps.
The same grass reaches out,

at the same spot, to tickle
the same fetlocks.
We approach that spot
where the girl will always tire,
and stretch her eyes back
in wonder
at all the covered distance.
She has no way of knowing
that the ride is not for her,
that we would capture our lame horse,
and set off along the stream,
and hope that this night
we would go far enough to hear
the moon whistle, or the grass croak,
or see the stream leave the borders
of earth like a woman
dropping her clothes,
go anywhere where the child's tired face
and the limp of the horse
can no longer contain us,
go anywhere where suddenly
we have grown into complete
understanding of the old folks' canon,
anywhere where the silent rainbow evening
has an answer to the crickets' song,
the gentle rain and a day so fierce
we dare not stare it down.

# THE SENSE OF COMEDY: I

Imagine yourself,
in the suit of lights,
strolling toward the barrier
as if you, alone, knew
the purpose of your coming.
You are suddenly erect,
suddenly the keeper
of a deeper knowledge.
You are suddenly another,
and yet yourself,
suddenly in control
of your own fear.
Right on time
without a sense of time,
you extend your hand
to become less private.
You turn to the stillness
of all these old
identifications.
Everything must be won again.
A clear call.
And the comedy begins, again.

# THE MUSEUMS IN CHAPULTEPEC

As round and soft as women,
they lie in the sun,
jealous coquettes tossing their kisses
under the feet of wire bulls,
Moore's concrete apples,
Giacometti's daggers.
Each afternoon, their cool chatter
freezes the flippant air,
and lovers, with warm eyes,
crawl to their sides with suspicious smiles.

# WALKING CHAPULTEPEC

These gardens circle up,
and lose you.
You can hear the call
of forbidden hunting
going on under you.
Every tree has a dull eagle
fixing you with his impertinent eyes.
A man in white invites you to a fountain,
where another, with cancer-eaten jaws
quaking like the gills of a fish,
swims toward your leg.
You walk where nothing will release you,
and only your tenacious separateness
will convince you that you are dreaming.

## MEETING HER IN CHAPULTEPEC

I would take you
wherever the provinces
dabble in paseos,
and the Sundays run in the sun
to the rhythm of your heart.
There, I'd go beyond
the sophistication of your dress,
your city manners, all those
smart denials in your eyes.

I look at your rich, brown body,
your polished hair, a covey
of frightened blackbirds
grouped at your shoulders,
and I know my decomposed Spanish
isn't good enough.
How shall I enchant your ears,
and make those African eyes
lie softly on your cheeks?

I watch you move,
remembering dances,
and think that I can chant
in Yoruba Lucumí.

# INSIDE CHAPULTEPEC CASTLE

Wherever you turn,
the sensual halls caress you.
Rose blood heroes snarl
and careen from the walls.
Jades and silver medals enchant your eye.
Fading amber tapestries and gold furniture
lie jealously next to them.

To get here,
you are pulled from below,
a baptized sinner,
emerging from the water,
still trembling.

If you listen,
you can hear something
picking at this temple's heart.
If you are still,
you can see a girl,
as pure as a goddess
who would embrace the chosen,
lie down to caress it.

# THE BIRTHDAY

My mind,
a child's again,
is filled with all your gifts.
I sit all night,
with the light out,
my back to the darkness
and my eyes kept focussed
at one point in the light,
as though I would fix
the face and name of a friend
absent even from my memory,
as though, by fixing that spot,
I could hold its heat against
the whispers of the shadows around me.
You have smiled,
and gone off to bed,
clamping your silence down
over the brilliant surprises
you hold for me.
Now, alone in the darkness,
I recall and memorize
the cards and telegrams
that came as early and polite
as unfamiliar guests,
their eyes picking out
my wrinkles and hesitations.
I am, it seems,
between one day and another,
between one age and another,
waiting in a time when only time
itself is the gift,
waiting in a darkness
I construct for the light.
How will I measure the movement now?

How will I know at what hour
to call you,
to clear this impossible stillness?
I am, it seems,
still moving toward the first light,
a chosen point to celebrate
the fact of moving still.
Before morning, you will be here,
and all strata and all mysteries,
and the music of the moon
that will establish me here
with your one impossible gift.

# JASON VISITS HIS GYPSY

This babbling gypsy
tosses beads at your feet,
and dares you to kneel
and grope before her.
You must keep your eyes
on her eyes,
on her hands,
on her body,
all at once,
and stop your ears, at first,
to her laughter and her talk.
It seems that she has been to school
near the dark edges of rivers;
or off at the end of a dog's howl
deep in a covered wood,
smashing her tambourines,
shoulder to shoulder,
with women who had learned tongues
in the middle of the ride;
or on some Sunday,
walked into a clapboard church,
lured by the coded stomp
of a righteous man.
It is no trick of beans
that leap from point to point,
or the click of some unruly syllable
that catches you.
You couldn't kneel
to gather a string of fallen beads
that you could purchase
from a ragman's cart,
for these.
Reduced to stillness,
you wait.

And now, at evening,
in a soft rain,
the desert at the gypsy's door
falls and lies like a loose and motley cloth.
The babble about you stops.
Only the flame of the kerosene lamp moves.
And now, the gypsy moves,
raveling the sand into her sleeve,
past your still body,
past your stilled desires.
Long ago,
when you entered this room,
with its scent of faded roses
and chicken fat,
with its shadows standing at attention
among the rasping curtains,
you signed with your eyes
the pact, from which you could not
be released into anything but silence,
from which you could not be released
until you had been cleaned
of all desires but one.
The gypsy knows what you have forgotten,
knows even what you would forget,
knows the rhythm of raveling
the sand into the dark and closeness
of a space, where only she can live,
waiting for those who need to kneel
again before the chosen and the strange,
leaving the unlucky omens of their lives
at the door,
to listen for distant voices and the knock
of ancestors grown weary from neglect.

# THE DEATH OF AN UNFAMILIAR SISTER

Your body,
measured out by moans,
lies, facing the unused patio,
in a room stripped of all
but your white-gowned bed.
All day and night,
the neighbor women shawl themselves,
and enter as quiet as awed lovers,
and beat themselves into remorse
and love of you.
I have been out of your life for years,
but find myself, miraculously found,
here on the floor among them,
unable to pray, or shout, or cry,
unable even to enchant myself
with the dark and unintelligible oaths
the women utter into the stones.
Once, in a sullen Mexican town,
an old scholar drew himself even,
for a moment, with the Mexican horizon,
and snapped his heart against it.
For two days,
I lay against his bed,
his uncommon smell and ruffled skin
so close I could not move
unless I changed them.
The women came,
and, just as these,
sang in the pain of their memories
of death, in their future knowledge
of death, regarding me
as though I were one of their own,

or had passed, through my own pain,
into the perfect death before us.
I did not pray, nor shout, nor cry,
nor enchant myself even then,
but sat as comfortably with him
as I do here with you.
I turn my eyes to the women,
moving toward the holy expression
of their entrance here,
and know they do not lie,
know that they are right
to thrash themselves into remorse.
We will be here for hours,
in the dark,
your bed the candle
by which we watch
the changes in each other.

Sister, I have walked to here,
over this compassionate dust,
to wait in this moving light
for your last movement,
the one movement
that these others will not
and cannot understand.
Their singing fervently rises;
it is the pitch and tone of our
forgotten spirits,
rising over this unfamiliar room.
Caught in it,
I ask for the blessing you cannot give,
and I know you will leave me alone at last,
with only this earth's touch, the women's silence,
but know, too, that the lid will close,
unveiling my one imperishable star.

# HOMECOMING

*Guadalajara–New York, 1965*

The trees are crystal chandeliers,
and deep in the hollow,
a child pits its voice
against the rain.
The city screams its prayers
at the towers in the distance.

Those guitars again.
And the Catholic mantis
clutching at the sky,
a pearl of a city,
cuando se duerme.

Subway blue boys
now ride shotgun
against my freedom and my fears.
Pistols snap like indignant heels,
at midday, and we stand at the docks,
singing a farewell we'd soon forget.

Hymns resound against that dome
entre la fiesta y la agonía.
Worms feed on its concrete,
or we pluck them out of bodies.

But time to forget.
Or remember the easiness
of leaving easy loves,
disappearing
in the arms of secret dreams.

We'll sit at the end
of a banquet board,

and powder our tutored wigs,
flip the pages of gentility
in the rainy season.
English lessons over tea
for the price of memory.

Il mio supplizio
è quando
non mi credo
in armonia.

They say the time
is not much different.
The strange and customary turns
of living may coincide.

In Mariachi Plaza
travelers sing elegies to the beauty
of revolutions and tranquillity.

From the opposite side of the river,
coming in, the sky line seems scrubbed
and pointed ominously into the darkness.

I walk through the market,
kissing colors in a murmur
of self-induced petition.

Two spires,
lying against the night,
are suddenly armed to sail.

The water foams against the bottom,
the way it looked when I left
that dying city.

Only a turning to feel the bark
slope off into the night,
with a promise to return.

> Un dì, s'io non andrò sempre fuggendo
> di gente in gente, mi vedrai seduto
> su la tua pietra, o fratel mio, gemendo
> il fior dei tuoi gentili anni caduto.

From line to line,
from point to point,
is an architect's end of cities.

But I lie down
to a different turbulence
and a plan of transformation.

# FROM
# *EXPLICATIONS / INTERPRETATIONS*
# (1984)

# TWENTY-TWO TREMBLINGS OF THE POSTULANT

## (Improvisations Surrounding the Body)

I

*1 (arm)*

Candles, ribbons and a cross
gaud my sash and tux.
My derby and white gloves
stand erect over my coffin.
This music greets death,
the winking, prancing lid
that lies
still with longing
for a bone that has flared,
an embryo with the power to appear.

*2 (forearm)*

Between
the hand and these long bones,
eight bones,
as small as covenant stones,
lie and turn about.
Articulate grip,
such force,
a god's delicate disguise,
alters the marks of the altar stones.

*3 (shoulder blade)*

Companioned pity, doubt's
double contradiction
reveal

the body's incisive intent.
Cut and placed just so,
they would seem to turn
                    from sun to moonrise,
each state and figure carefully defined.
Caulicle scribes of heaven's notice,
they graph love's
              irradiant positions.
Under the head's strict account,
the body's lost arc and arch
count the platelets in love's force.

*4 (fingers)*
*for Albert Ayler*

Patron of a dap,
            a dapper sound,
let us here recall
breath,
presence
and desire.
Witch moss listens for the elephant horn,
the dirge of imprisoned light.
Darkness charges your bell's light;
its emptiness endures
                  in your free light,
point without closure,
space without beginning.
Your fingers must endure
        the astringent eyes
              your horn wears.

IV

*5 (thigh)*

To him who has not killed
it is forbidden to drink
                    the virgin's beer.
Sun and son of the thigh mark
must press the distance
        deeper into the spirit's grip.
                    You sail,
                    shorts slit so high
                    the cloth billows
                    and rides
                    around your waist.
This stadium veils the paradigm of the race;
the wood obscures the declension of the hunt.
Your tempered thighs, contesting air,
                  unfurl love's amber presence.

*6 (tibia)*

Your father guards the story in a cedar box:
a vulture's tracks, fish bones, a cattle head,
discarded mat, sheared pot, the forgotten
dispositions that empowered your music.

The dry north calls the whistle and whisper
of a darkened cave from Muslim mouths.
You have returned with your bleached, marrowed
bone, home of the god's throat,
            embedded
in the flute certainty,
            in the midnight
of the cave's red, comforting leaves.

## I

*7 (foot)*

Even at night,
a trace of sunlight hangs in the east.
Air creates an immobile, blue canticle.
The seagulls' incapable wings remain
"merely an unwithering tumble,
a chute of angels fallen
by a sheer delight in their weight."
You set out in the delight of a fall.
Flight's image defines
        the conjunction of your besieged foot
with the zodiac of a timeless god's
                                weightless grief.

*8 (lower jaw)*

Dressed and belled in perfect order,
we arrive under the tomb sound,
the antiphonal knock of the smith.
We have enshrined the speaker's ninth hour,
harmony's impulse, in visible acts.
The knife's deep exaltation settles
the mouth's thirty-two degrees, exults
the votive articulation of the unspeakable.
Our stripped gifts of measure and control
begin the descent of the shuddering,
                                        communal jaw.

## V

*9 (toes)*

Disguised,
I walk by night
and listen for the rain.

It slips upon and shakes
these blue white nameless wings.
The rumor of roses, gossip of foxgloves
remember death's cause.
Night refuses to fit the cluster
of cobblestones, bees' lamps,
a woman's scented and magic pot.
The rain in the bird's wings, the antelope's
certain hoofbeat raise the dead
          at the moment of rest.
I must remember to discover
the unfamiliar terrain of my shadow,
the doṅu bird's scale in my toes
          on the ground.

*10 (anus)*

Why should you come,
    with your voice filled
        with the morning's bright oranges,
to be saddled and hiccuped into pleasure?
Love dresses, in this room,
    in the wrong color.
        I light
cold water in a porcelain bowl
to cover the swiveled space
    the barbed god left us.
Five yams, five kola nuts, two logs
    of firewood from the ita tree.
Junior wife of the road,
I have sponged holiness
    into the room's extended body.
Now you must touch my deepest disguise
    and pray for an uncorrupted star,
        the light of an uncontaminated ship.

I

*11 (nose)*

The dignity in beaten maize abrades the nose.
Brute heat rises, weed strong, above the lake's decline.
Shellfish embrace the moon disc on the shore.
Our memory of passage lodges in a goatskin,
                                        lashed to a rock.
Night breathes in a crystal purity
and in the sleep of comfort in burnt cactus.
We descend,
                    from the sun's point,
on the red liquid of exchange.
The cocoa smell of cayenne fills the desert
and assures us that the cut will heal,
the scar will disappear.

*12 (mouth)*

Six o'clock.
Blanketed and muffled,
we circle the reclining forest,
through the morning's guard
of drooping banana leaves,
cacti, clumps of grass,
    dead rhododendrons.
                    Conjure
a cedar stump for your hand
and a likeness in a cradled, scented body.
If silence is the forest's majestic word,
the name it invokes at dawn,
the mouth must be bridled,
until the tree has understood
    its canon death in the carver's song.

I

*13 (hair, head and neck)*

Near dawn, she purls through the brush
to appear, sibilant and serene, at the elder's blueberry stream.
Midwife of God's unbroken hour,
she cuts his morning body for the stars,
lotus, doṅu bird, calabash and stolen seed,
all the fiction of his craft and command.
Her plaited, pearled hair now measures
danger's intervals in a heron dream,
the reptilian night, in a virginal return,
a death without end.
She has taught me the limits of contemplation
and the way a bone,
        though it be taken from the truest cross,
                                                  decays.
I have it from her conch in the water's web:
high tribulation attends every celebratory bell.
I know now, my woman will bell down berries
at the water's edge, to press a devotee's
uneasiness into my traveling bones.

*14 (chest)*

I know this country by the myth of the rose,
those linden tenors, lilting swords, unruly loves,
larcenous runts who rise from the mist at the peak
of an insurmountable passion.
I have been given the book of a peasant heart
and the cave for a passion other than my own.
I would acknowledge my journey
                                            down
                                the decent path
                        of tenure, here to the grammar of being,
standing-in-itself, arising, enduring,
the radical exegesis of the false myth of existence.

Sausage dark blood piques my thirst again
for the intemperate sword and jackboot love
my body holds for itself.

*15 (stomach)*

I would have you an unblemished bell,
an angular assertive god, text for the perfect
singer in the perfect grove
or carve you
in ebony or sandstone, a toucan perched in an ebony
bowl in a corner of this room.
You understand the danger of being stripped
of totem and amulet, the bliss of being cold
to a god's stroke and set, untangled,
darkened in wisdom, in the direction of a self
you may never reach.
A migratory man, licked by the serpent,
you dug your life from under withered baobab,
became your own, a seventh, son.
I turn and turn. You remain.
You have taken your insatiable appetite
away from the limits of our love.

*16 (ear)*

Pagan by birth, you arrange your route by spring.
You bring your eastern, skitterish saw to cradle us into night.
For days, you boil us in hymns,
stopping only to admire your wife, in white
from heel to head, stutter into tongues
or stagger into dance.
We raise you into prophecy and offer you
this house, the left-over moments of ecstasy,
the right to pierce our hearts with your fluent saw.
All night, the women clasp the serpent's sting
and reel uncertainly after your melodies,

into your wife's design or into inventive glosses
upon your meager lexicon.
This, too,
is the watch for that star's spin, the seed's turn.
This, too, is the ear open
to the accumulation that begins our death.
Strange, how you, having taught an element to sing,
come unmasked, riding the morning into night,
invoking the music which binds you to this place,
able to distinguish what little can be spoken,
or what space the silence leaves
to redeem our souls.

## IV

*17 (sides)*

Come sunset you can bet
like a moth at a flame
old Blind Man will be here
cue caught up in his crotch
cup of Mr. Boston cuddled
under a corner of the table

take a nickel more
if you can run six
before he get a line
got such an eggplucking touch
young men close their eyes and sleep
stand at his side          and learn

money down mouth back
come light          beef up
hey          take a nickel on a run
who want to shoot the Blind Man one

buy a drink          you will.

*18 (spinal column)*

High in the wind,
Chinese gongs quiver in the night.
It is winter.
All day I play with your fig wine vision
and tamper with the tricks love has taught my tongue.
Here, I have a moment to construct the path you set me.
I am at bells' end,
buckled in the shift you spur.
I have truckled to the arks and bright beds
of virgins who could not be clear.
Let me tell you of the wickedness of spring
and the giddy danger of unthreading a maze.
I know, and regret, the moon's embrace
of the straightbacked, nubile sun.

I

*19 (kidneys)*

In time,
in tune and omen rich,
I spin about my body,
at ease with my sabbath temper.

I know there is a mark
upon the man who only knows
a penitent's shiver at a Joshua tree,
whose only peace is

intoxicated stillness,
or the breath of holiness
that comes when evil, faced,
has been denied.

But what can we deny,
when each body falls,

plump with his father's gifts,
into this body already rich

with the god's gifts?
Your shepherds now shiver under these bells.
They stamp about our feet
and pinch their fingers at our mouths.

Disguised,
I rise, under your eyes, from dung,
to begin my trembling.
My eyes remember

the goat's quiver,
my purity's star-bound blood,
the liver-laden word
in its moon cold silence.

Redeemed, I keep
longing's mark on my body.
Just once I turn away,
finding these fathers' gifts

too much to bear.

### *20 (clavicle)*

My dancing master of the gold bead,
I see you trouble the waters
        between that moment of light
and the star's darkness.
                                        Doubled
in your body, you wake; you twist,
then lurch, your body into motion.
Played upon by love's one breath,
you mount your antelope, the horse
who releases the cull bone god in you.

You anoint me the coffin's scribe.
A second birth folds us head to head.
Death doubles us to ride
        earth's sunken ark
toward a second and hazardous light.
Master, remember it was you,
discontent with your own imitation,
who frayed and made these bones delicate
        by bathing them in time.

V

*21 (back of the hand)*

Light,
night's unladen image
in your wedding dress, the thin line
erasing heaven's darkness,
staunches me in its shadow.

All night,
I feel you smack my cheek
and wake me to the thunder
of your breathing,
                a mother's moan,
a bride's clamor for rain.

Surgical,
you could part my body
along earth's axes; spirit me
among your father's oaths and altars.

I belong to the figure
        of the rain
you coil with your hand,
the stones that find
their places only at your touch.

If I awake, with you,
in darkness, it is the clean
incision of your love
that calls the light to dance,
just out of reach,
        on earth that rises
                clearly
without the press of your hand.

*22 (eye)*

Ecstatic, full,
and still half-blind,
I see you clear your body
of its scars.
                    Astonished
by the magic of my name,
I name your scars, the angry cuts
stitched and hidden from yourself.
How shall we measure these bleached bones?
How shall we disregard the curry of a prophetic fox?
All peace is stolen,
        a disfigured rite,
nourished by your scars and breathless denials.
Those others now know my name.
Yet how can we possess
what you yourself have lost?
We own no land,
no love, no art, no death.
We walk among these signs of your
dispossession
and hear you say you passed this way,
like this,
            and it was right.

(The last two bars are tacit.)

# LOVE'S DOZEN

## THE RITUAL TUNING

Now I will enter the house of affliction.

King carry me above myself in death.
Awake to the king of all,
I come, regal in my purpose,
out of the heated darkness.
Tune me only now;
I tune myself to your love
and your many-eyed longings,
to your deepest look into your life.

I am the contradictions that you make me.
Scaled, I climb your trees.
I lay my eggs, one by one,
and suckle them.
And in my sign I raise
the bright seed of my spirit.

I am two heads in one,
two lives in one.
I end my life in a double vision.
When I am eaten, you pass
this double deed among yourselves.

Love is to enter another's house
a creature coined from vision's deepest pain.

Here, creature of heaven,
I surround you with my sign,
and look upon your marriage bed,
and look upon your death.

## Love in the Water, Love in the Stone

Faithful bean lady of the plantain,
your tubular beads surround my voice.
You bring me a berry song so old
I hug the silences. You
embrace the silence and the clear light
on the track of your quest, to here.
I see now in that light myself
into the tangle of the river's bottom.

Knee-deep in another's bliss,
I wake and find myself a stone
at your lover's feet.
Then stone upon stone,
I rise into another's fire.
I touch your palm oil flesh
to light me from my cave.
And, if I rise, under your thunder,
into rain, I praise your touch.

Now, life-long a laterite,
a rain of beads, palm kernel oil
stipulate my clipped time.
The earth weaves eight gold bridal veils
to cast into the sea. The moon
is up at noon to catch me naked,
drunk and dancing with a ram.
I use the loom of seasons so;
I abuse myself.
And, even if I leave you,
I marry your worship in my wife's voice.

I begin the decline of having you
close;

your memories feed me.
These are my intolerable survivals.
And so I take my love's journey
from the language of your needs.
I mount my woman's earth smell
in the shadows of your ageless eyes.
I crawl to the altar of your thunderstones
and bleed for the bride whose blood
will fill my name.

## Love in the Iron and Loom

Double the earth in northern light;
double the west in water.
Twin me in iron and weaving.
Binu, Lébé, my male hand
knows my woman's hardness.
I am the twin of my head, the twin of my hand.
Woven into cloth,
I slither from the dance a mask.
I am a dance in mask.
Who will answer the figure of the dance?
Who will unmask the twin at my heart?
My water shape in stone has a grip
upon the earth.
My river has a line around the star.
Shuttle and hammer, my life coheres.
My axe is the altar stone,
the loom of your love.
I know you as my cold light,
and as my dying light,
and as the barking star I ride
through love's light.
My lord's light is the deep pit
of my marriage bed,
the song of my sign within the dance.
Weep, weep, weep.
Brother mask, you leap
to double me from myself.
I am broken.
I am finished.
I weep for the twist of my craft
in the green river of my god's love.

## Love as Heaven's Nostalgia

Rhine moonstone, light
of the devastated world,
I could name your nobleness
in minerals and stars,
or in the light's courage.
Yet in my ear the ages linger.
I know your passion for a melody,
your nostalgia for heaven.
I wait, under your touch,
for the vision of your governing.
Sisters, I will awaken in myself
your melodic temper.
Strange how my life runs down to reason
in the memory of a bright daughter;
I am at the gate of a lost life;
I am at the door of my own harmony.
And you, delivered from this world,
summon my purified soul to sit
in its nature with the stars.

## Anagnorisis

Through blood
and into blood
my spirit calls.
You sit at my head
and weave my power.
Queen, I do not do as you
and deal in deaths.
I have no power to make
that male power crawl to my knees.
Yet I speak and am your seer,
chaste lover and your bridge
                    from the dead one's
blackened space
to the white sun of your prayer,
the red demon of your mother love.

You took the crescent moon and named me.
You bought my axe and sent me
through the desert of my southern dreams.
Clearly, in my sign,
I love
your overburdened body.
I love you
as the black chapel
                    of my penitence.
I love your forest's touch
in winter's memory.
Now, I grapple your deeds to my tongue.
And out of your woman's common eye,
I take my son's pursuit
of the days he must live
                              to recall.

## Transcendent Night

Your feather hands
are love's nest in winter,
and yet I fly,
or do I dream I fly.
And I would fly
to nestle near your child's lake,
to press my needs upon your feather hands.
There at the lake,
in the shadow of the celt
I find there,
I dance in your spine's darkness;
I clothe you in your spirit's darkness
and in your body's darkness.
I awake to the light of your total darkness.
I keep, for my constant spring,
your feather hands upon my eyes.
My eyes will always take
the dark path to your heart.
My heart will drink its light
from the only heavy hands
                    you offer me.
Death of the dark. Death of the light.
I live in my spirit's web of love's
            transcendent night.

## Love in the Weather's Bells

Snow hurries
the strawberries
from the bush.
Star-wet water rides
you into summer,
into my autumn.
Your cactus hands
are at my heart again.
Lady, I court
my dream of you
in lilies and in rain.
I vest myself
in your oldest memory
and in my oldest need.
And in my passion
you are the deepest blue
of the oldest rose.
Star circle me an axe.
I cannot cut myself
from any of your emblems.
It will soon be cold here,
and dark here;
the grass will lie flat
to search for its spring head.
I will bow again
in the winter of your eyes.
If there is music,
it will be the weather's bells
to call me to the abandoned chapel
of your simple body.

## The Crosses Meet

Patiently, I set your seat
in cedar and a bit of gold,
and by its arms
I cross our lives.
And then I turn your body
toward the wind,
my path from worship
to certainty.
Now, may I house
my woman's meaning
in angels and in stone.
I hold this pagan three-in-one
under your lips
and under your last sign.
Could, now, I trade
your daemons for her body,
I would cut the hardwood
of your seat to peace.
But can you hear me
when I press my preservation
at her knees,
and leap from the tangle
of your seated cross
to the bell of my own voice
at her worship?
You hear me
as I walk from dark
                                        to dawn
to save you.
And so I do save you
when my voice
is at her service.
I serve and preserve myself
in her grace.

I sit her on the tangled
stool of grace.
I take her voice alone
to rule in my politic body.
At last your crosses meet
in the love above love,
in the word that spells itself
                                        in silence,
and I am the carpenter
of your new spirit
that speaks to hear itself
                                        in stone.

## Love Plumbs to the Center of the Earth

1

I will live with winter
and its sorrows.
Here, the earth folds its blanket
at noon.
The eastern crown appears,
disappears,
appears
to lie in pine
on the west ridge.
Some light has been lost;
a stillness has been betrayed.

I seem to feel your body
shake that stillness through the deep
water which separates us now.
Your husband, my father,
plumb of the earth
from our air to his,
lies in the silence of water
we gave to him.

You say you sit at night afraid,
and count the gifts you carried
to his bed.
I know that they contain
this fear of the winter's sorrows,
this offense of being left above
the deep water
to pluck this plumb string
for a tremor of love.
But it isn't the melody of loss

you have in your moon bucket,
nor the certainty of a line
to your own pain.
The clamor that rides this line
unhinges sorrow,
unburdens its beatific companions.
This single string,
a heart's flow,
is a music of possession.
And so you twin me
in the plain song of survival,
in the deep chant of winter
and its own sun.
Our balance is that body
and the sun extended
from our grief.

2

Today,
nine days
after the hunters have gone,
a buck walks from the forest,
and nuzzles at my snow-heavy trees.
I crown him king of the noon,
and watch the light drip from his coat.
In these woods,
his light is a darkness,
an accommodation with winter
and its mid-day shroud.
And, if at night, the moon
holds down its spoon cup,
he will be fed by light
that holds the darkness in it.
His body is the plumb line
the stars shake upon our earth.
Now, will I dare to follow

and to name his steps
through every darkness of our earth,
or shall I turn from that light
to my own winter's light?

3

Left. Right.
Turn. And counterturn.
I would have my foundation stone.
And so I carefully turn my words
about your longing.
Soil, water, root and seed,
the pin of light on which your love
will ride to air finds and turns
in the heart of each of its possessions.
You own me in the grief
you will not bear,
and in the act you will not name.
You crown my darkness in your silence,
and you crown me king of my engendered light.
If I possess a seat to rule,
I rule love's coming and the taut
sound of my father's voice in you.
Voices of that deep water stretch
into heaven on a thin line filled
with all we do not possess.

## The Unwedding of the Magdalene of the Vine

Down, on your bare feet,
with a wicker basket of tomatoes,
you come to the courtyard of blue roses,
rare garden on a rare day,
and you are pinioned in the waterfall
from which the day would seem to rise.
I rise on the curl of your hair into ecstasy;
my love boat knocks from shore to dark green shore.
The birds go braying where I hide
                                        my intaglio of you.
This is my Mary lock and locket,
my chalice and the box I will not open.
Clearly, you have pruned me from your vines.
I know you through the earth's rising
and through the candles which you light
at your grandmother's grave.
Your red fruit defines a day you took from her bones,
sets my limits, calls my wedding bells.
Magdalene of the vine,
I would be free of the wicker of your day's duty,
your barter bays from dawn to twilight.
But in the waterfall's night, I hear you
call your familiar faces against me.
A Jesus of my continent veils your voices.
I am at rest as a shaker of serpents.
I once had a dervish depth to dapple you.
I once had my love's sorrow
                                        to draw you near me.
Now, I follow you down the sunshine,
and know the blood of the earth in the fruit,
the white pull of your bones upon the earth.
Now, here, I take the waterfall to wash
this stain of marriages from me.

I will not have you as my duty to the earth,
nor take the white pull of your bones
to reason with my days.
I have pitted your bare feet and wicker basket
against the jealous redness of my stripped love.
Unwed, I accept your turning of this our earth.

## Love's Coldness Turns to the Warmth of Patience

My blanket smells of burnt apples.
My hair is tangled in smoky birch.
I sleep. I wake to watch the snow
ease itself around the shivering hills,
the same ice tick off in islands on the lake.
In all these silent postures,
I burrow into the memory of winter,
and fall, past your warmth,
into the high air of your heart.
Now, I am with you when the birds
circle and redeem their own air
and press the sun to hide their losses
in rainbows and serpent skins,
and, while you read their Zeno's flight,
I read your stillness.
I see now
in your eye the birds are bronzed
to be set near our temples in the wood.
Water and bronze, the birds curled on a staff
lead me to the purity of my own coldness,
down where what is lit is still unseen
and the blind light is the token
of your only star.
For who hopes for what he sees?
But if we hope for what we do not see,
we wait for it in patience.
I wait for the turning to teach me
what can be seen and what,
as I sit near my north star,
my lost green wood reveals.
I take the clothing of my memory's winter
as a sign that you are patient still.

Surely, I am my own flight into stillness
and into the cadence of a necessary cold.
I comfort you in the bed of charity,
my soul redeemed in your body's expected fire.

## New Adam's Cross

Dove, I offer you my hand,
and, from my shadows,
try to contain your sacred flight.
If I can name you or your flight,
I contain you. Berry lady,
I say love is your succulence.
Or are you my moonfall at the waterfall?
I know you are the blue bead
and the chicken kick, the diamond
or the gold stuck upon my stool.
At noon, I hear your frothy roll
bleat upon my grove's shores.
You come in the rain, you come in the wind,
you come in the eastern star; rose and redhead,
lily of the desert, my balm and blackness,
you surround me with your signs
and with your perfect body.
If now I am Adam,
you are my Eve of morning
and yet you cannot take your form
from my desire or from the gods' design.
I know my lure is useless.
I know I lie in shadows
because I cannot see your true light.
I say all light appears in darkness,
and every body rises against emptiness.
I say I know you through your mother
and my uncertain knowledge of her body
and her spirit. I know you as the web of my
father's spirit's weave and caress you
as the infinite water sign you weave.
Is love the name you weave?
And do I stand in the white milk of dawn
with only a red star for a sign

and watch my only horse split the air
and watch you wave your benediction at our backs?
And through your transparent body
can I see old palm leaves become
my first dwelling,
my first altar stone,
my first bride's first bed,
my fire,
my first grave?
Do I see you as the first example of my being,
or as the oldest road I take into my being?
You are the cross my body hangs
upon its spirit, the light my eyes will take
to read these oldest questions.
I am not all of you, you draw away from me.
I break my unillumined bones.

## Love as the Limit and Goal

What in me is best
I lead to the hard stone
under the sun,
or to the dark habitation
of the blessed dead
where love's music
will be cut from my ear,
my body laid to serve
a constant light.
The subject of my own desire,
I am egg and synapse,
the body's pulsing measure,
the gold and purple of the light
about my days.
And so I invest myself,
invest you, with all
by which I dispossess you.
Now, when I beat my temple drum
and shake my bell
and praise my love in you,
I see the altar lock its heart
against your ecstasy.
The burden of the key,
under the rainbow,
rides you still.
You take the corn
for the thread of your skirt.
Love is the limit and the goal
by which that death is measured.
This love is the kinship of the saints
we bleed to make us worthy.
I turn from the order
of this constant dispossession
to awaken my body to the spirit's

historical sign, the logic of my soul
enlightened by your grounded eye.
I turn from possession of your oneness
to the vision of your twin acts,
the breaking of the ground from which I rise,
invested with the light my grave reveals.

# INSCRUTABILITY

1

Inscrutable when I speak,
I am learning how my body sounds.
In the sand by the river's edge,
my head is a moon's egg,
my shell is a bell in my boat.
My arms and legs are storms.
I turn left, I turn right.
I chain myself with sun's rays,
star spur coals, bits of coal diamonds
and granite, a yucca branch,
a chicken claw and rose thorn;
I stretch goat hide between my arm and chest,
balata and steel from my lips,
and laud my women near the water.
The song I hear refers me to the mark
upon my body.
I hear my death again in nail rings.
I set the nail as harp of my breath.
Such music can be measured.
We have, then, a measure of zones
and generations, the association
of cloth and iron, herring bones and keys,
and, if I take my malt to the garden,
the glass contends with maguey,
the beads of crown and sceptre
recall an ascetic quarry.
But, temple bar, I inquire
how I am to examine you.
I have a measure for the facts,
but none for you.
Though I live in the essential
condition of vision,
what truth I know

is a burden in my ear,
sign and countersign
of the light's discoveries.
Light is a weight in the ear,
a memory of the light's incisions,
and, in the dark, I clear
my possession of memory's poles
with the attributes of speech.
Then, if the god speaks of failure,
I tune my body's speech star-high.
I work the dead from darkness
into light; for these
there is no other definition.
Darkness and silence define
a lover on a bed,
or shuttled in a tree,
a constellation of beads,
bridal veils and berries.
I hear in the contradiction
of my song, a weeping.
My speech is a plumb line
to the echo of the earth.
My voice survives on a dervish dance,
and a king's howling body
would be the first stone of my house.
These are the deeds
to possession of my body;
these are the acts
by which I dispossess myself.
I remain a morph in my own
proposition.
Clearly,
my leaving and return
are in my power.
I number my powers
by an inscrutable class—
my voice in the leaves of a river
in which my light and full

and silent body lies.
I ask how to measure
the leaving and return,
the weight of the body.
I ask which of the marks I must
perceive to enhance my speaking.
I examine, now, the exactness
of salvation, proverb and purpose,
the blaze of the serpent skin.
I am persuaded of spring oats
and corn and barley, wine
and sweetmeats, darkness
and this text on light and the dark.
I speak only what is sufficient
and what can be assured
by the essential condition of vision.
I am in the place of light,
a bell in my own boat,
storm-driven into speech,
and, by the rhythm of desire,
I forge my body's space.
I refer to the unity of this space,
and to my body's singular paradigm.
But even here, I wait with you
for the bird's flight into meaning.

2

*(i)*

This must be said.
I am provoked by the state of things.
On the most propitious night,
the mother claims her god's
singular visit; the results
are the birds you see before you.
Bird, I know you as a common thief
of fish, a puller of nets in the dawn.

You cannot fly by your hungers.
But the god assures your holiness.
Our speech assures your struggle
with the god; your body addresses
this schema of our own desires.
You are the rain's head, the solitary
prayer in the brass-filled temple,
the mutilated tree on the rainless hills.
If you are silent,
we turn that silence to a tilling tool,
an eave, a hearth, or a pot.
We wear your silence against the heat.
We tune our day's bells to your pauses.
Your every proposition is grace,
a perfection of our absences.
Twin, you title all my voiceless provocations.
And yet I am indifferent to the terms
you choose, until I choose them.
Changer, fox, a fallen verb,
even you provoke my speech.
I ignore your generation.
Determined,
I begin again to parse my body's needs.
I ask if the world is real enough
to measure my intention.

*(ii)*

Down where the smallest quality
will turn and figure itself,
turn again to become other than itself,
I hear the exact belling of my vexation.
(Strange, how I refer to every act as sound.)
I body all my logic of the world
in the gray depths of these changes.
I pull the world's bare figures
to the scaffold of my gray eye.
I am, in the form of my own urging,

my gray eye and, in its movement,
I have my schemes, my launch-pad
into the actual.
If the god's elemental bones are real,
my hand must never scruple to design his flesh.
Old men will have it
that the word alone is real,
and leave these facts in pieces.
Is the word the design of the fragments,
or of the strict connection of the missing fact?
Surely, a yeoman would search another tree,
or the leaf fallen from the same tree.
Thing is not a name, and a tree
is named by virtue of its life.
You must consider that the tree has changed.
The tree alone can never bear semblance
to such a stripped body.
I assert now the eye is a pauper;
crown it, and subtract the self.
The English, impersonal banker retreats,
is content, is at home, is heard no more.
If I am intelligible as the other,
I explore my body's future path.
I become the body's changing form,
transformed by any unspoken absence.
The act itself is figure and ground
for the necessary absence.
Then we must go down,
through the will of the dead,
and ride the living mind to the dance
of light, distinguish the tune
in which our names are called.

*(iii)*

Still, I am entranced
by the eye's harmonics—
soundings of the invisible;

historical return;
field of the line and counterline;
false note and true;
house of fact and composition;
sphere in the wall of two lights.
Old opposites possess me once again.
I surrender and contest
my power to enhance you,
my need to embrace you as you are.
Are you the ring in the peacock's tail,
the round stone temple on an arid
mountain, the black belly of a fish
in moon rings? Are you a footprint
glazed on the urn of the sand,
the litter-shield of a warrior's body,
a bride in a white hut,
the drum or its message of love?
Voiceless rainbows speak in their colors.
The wind rides its horse
up the cobbled streets at noon.
Up, down. All figures rise or fall.
They arrive before me.
They remain.
I remain, a sinew in an aggressive hip,
the counterweight to another speaker's
exultant eye.
You must adjust to this intensity.
In the tumult of this body's vision,
I must elicit my intention.

*(iv)*

I am arguing with the body's exaltation
and the mind's enstoolment on the seat of love,
all inebriate devices of the fallen.
I cling to the fate of taking one step
at a time, or so I say, and know I lie.

I lie by the process of enacting my memories.
You are in these acts.
I cite your losses; I cite your powers.
We devise the truth of all
                                        we have not learned.
It has been given to us to understand
what may only be spoken.
What is unspoken may be undone,
what is undone may be unspoken.
I am proposing the clarity
of the undone, the still unspoken,
the clarity of stillness in the movement,
of the movement in the perfect calm.
I am proposing the undetermined body,
the invested space.
I cite the ages of liberation—
from the key,
from the second eye,
from sainthood
and from death,
from the body's definition
and its investment,
from the quality of being actual.
I bring you every disposition
of the double.
You will not find my sign
bare in your gray eye,
nor shivering feebly and alone
in your ear,
but bodied in the deep ground
of my tongue's impossible passage
through the ill-defined logic
of my body's exaltation.

FROM

*DIMENSIONS OF HISTORY*

(1976)

# THE EYE OF GOD,
# THE SOUL'S FIRST VISION

Brightness is a curse upon the day.
The light has turned the plain cave dark.

Who chooses me
to rise river-burdened, here,
where the sun has bent itself
and sprinkled ash about our doors?
To be a river spirit
I would have to burn this ash again
to moonrays and sunlight,
control the waves that push us higher
on the land.
I strain to clasp my dust again,
to make it mine,
to understand the claims the living
owe the dead.

Who burned this land,
and sent us evidence of the god's retreat?

Rain on the brow of the arid nurse of lions
is the ash from which I rise.
Emblems remembered in a rain forest
become my compass.
I am that head the little girls carry at their backs.
I am an angular bird,
dedicated to healing,
iron-wrought and ready to fly again.
I am that center of a star,
risen on the wings of empire,
the warm pit of auquénidos.

Like the master of the spear,
I cross my river now,
always to return to one beginning,
which may be one or no beginning.
Under the tightly bound arms
and the spirit of masks,
I return to you,
                    to name,
                         to own,
to be possessed and named myself,
following the movement of the eye of God,
whose lids will close upon your greater claims.

And so I start in search of that key,
the ankh,
that will unlock the act.

"Much I have strained to make my soul obey."
Not in the perfect understanding of submission,
my feeling given form
to ride upon your judgment.

Unusual lights are at our altars.
Unusual hands go 'round our pots,
and dip into the blood that we alone can shed.
But
      "I have made an end of my failings,
       I have removed my defects . . .
       I am purified in my double nest."

Is this only in death?

Where did I learn to present myself
to the cut of some other voice,

substitute in a mime
my body breaks to contain?

But
    "I have become a prince,
     I have become glorious,
     I am provided with what is necessary."

These are the signs of understanding
that I assert, but cannot reach alone.

"Sleep had carried me away a little while.
The first thing I did on waking was to take an omen:
whatever words and whatever magnificat
came into my heart, that I would know to be
the rising of a sign portending the return
of my spirit to my body."

I need not now create a goddess for this earth,
or name the earth in a's or flowers,
or in blinkered weekdays clamoring for rain.
My intent is not to fork the branch of a tree
and fill it with God's axe alone.
These acts must give rise
to the birth of a star,
whose understanding is our life among ourselves.

Yet
    "By my father I adjure you, this that I say comes
     from the continuance of calamity and the consequence
     of misery, from a heart that is stirred
     from its foundations and tormented with its
     ceaseless conflagrations, by itself within itself.
     For thus it is, being without perception, without

> speech, without feeling, without joy, without repose,
> without effort: not in the sense of passing away, but
> because it is constant in the calamity of ceaseless
> torment, a torment without meaning, past indication,
> beyond limit. . . . If it speaks, speech is an affliction;
> and if it is silent, silence is an affliction. Unto
> God is the complaint without complaining, and there
> comes no answering reply, no easing. So it continues,
> wholly swallowed up: in loneliness hidden, yet it
> appears, and is hidden, and appears, and is hidden.
> I know not what I say, nor what he says whose reins
> have fallen from him, whose straps have been severed;
> who wanders in most perilous wildernesses,
> and thereof has no share in the conditions of
> blessedness . . ."

My scope is not a god's,
but he has placed this sign of birds between us.
And did I wake to see
the sweet potato grapple with the fire,
eight days in transit from my beginning
to my fulfillment?
But I have learned that that is no fulfillment,
only the first death that I must suffer,
only the first acceptance of another goal,
the eye opening on a different order.
This is blood of my mother given bodily form,
spirit of my father, spear hand,
the opening ear,
the point at which I am myself,
                                        and yours.

It will be difficult
for me to lie at rest in my own suffering.
It would be a death that comes too soon
to deny the sight of things not seen,

the signs that plough these fields,
people these houses,
cut into these conflicts.

What trust has been forgotten?
"Tumi nyina wo asase so."
All power is in land,
on which you lie.

So red is the color of the day.
Young mother, you bleed too much.
You must reject your son.
So red is the color of the day.
Young mother, we will teach you
to thread your bowels about your blood.
Here is the red clay and the red mukula tree.
The hunters know these things,
and so will you now.
You must remember when you lay
in the place of death and suffering
how you accepted the teaching of the tree.
That tree's whiteness,
white as the beads draped on the bow
in your lonely hut,
white as your fertile womb,
taught you to hear the women,
playing on the little drum of thirst,
the hand up and down the reed,
the sound of love
from which your loneliness would retreat.
Dancing,
you carried your beads in a pack on your head.
Solemnly, one night,
you showed them to your husband
on your marriage bed.

Now, you bleed too much,
angry with our needs.
We dress you in hunter's skins,
fill your hands with bow and arrow,
turn you 'round in our hunter's dance.
There is a feather of a lourie bird above your brow.
Hunter,
manslayer,
circumciser,
you will not take your place.
Little mother,
remember our need.
Thread your bowels about your blood.
We are waiting to be moving again.

I cannot buy my brother's gifts,
nor can I buy a life.
But you see me, here,
waiting through my seasons,
with the accumulation
of all that we have suffered and won.
"I am not a man whom girls refuse."
At night,
I dream of the termination
of these searcher's feelings
and the day of rain, upon which
I shall begin to build myself again.
But here alone I sit
with the tassel and the bell,
holding the celebration of my people's love.
I can hear these bells in a distance,
and hear them shake the child's voice,
singing his ox's name in your womb.
We cut them to a peacefulness,
and breed them to witness
our slow coming together,

to bear the burden of the years
in which you will meet me
                                                  again and again,
each death a growth,
a life rising into its clarity of being,
a love unspoken when we shout our spears.
"Friend, great ox of the spreading horns,
whichever bellows amid the herd,
ox of the son of Bul
Maloa,"
teach me to hear
the tone of my child,
singing in the future history of my wife.

                                    Turn again
to the blood given bodily form.
I lead you down, little mother,
to the river of your dispossession.

In season thirst,
we dust the roads, and come
to rest only when the seed
pulls us into the earth,
or when, at the end of the long
battle of tides, its fruit appears,
and calls us from our wandering.
Then the boys leave your kitchens,
and beat the flies and stench
                                                  from their faces
to sneak into the pain and power
they will have to die into to know.
Again, mother, you must learn the lesson
of this sweet dispossession.
And now, little master of the dance,
we turn to you,

the reflection of the reasons we have
to straddle you before a knife
to cut you away from her
who would never but always possess you,
to teach you to bear the burden of our lives
within your own.
Who you are
and where you are
we teach you to teach us.
So I would wear myself
the feather of the lourie bird,
and be the hand to cut you
into this special kinship.
Yes, my little mother,
"I am the lion who eats on the path
You sleep on your back, you look into the sky
Nest of the marabout stork where a black kite lays eggs
Hole of a mamba where a lizard lays eggs
Novice's mother, you used to revile me
Bring me your child that I may mistreat him
Your child has gone
The son of a chief is like a slave."
Now, disguised, kambanji,
you ride another master
into your mother's exhilaration,
where she will soon learn the meaning
of another death.

If I possess these souls,
they are all that I have.
For you have given me this name,
and burdened me with memory and duty,
a tricky commerce with the dead deceivers,
the injured and the ambitious.
What I had you took
into the possession of this black stool.

What I receive
I pay in food or thanks.
If I lead against another,
I gain nothing but his tribute.
His gods will not fit in my stool house,
nor mine in his.
"Tumi nyina wo asase so."

Who has burned this land?
Who has sent me, shaven head,
bleeding for my princes?
Who has chosen me
to reconstruct this eye of God,
to understand the signs
                                        of this dispossession,
to slip, beyond this pain, this key in the lock
to objectify this joy?

# RHYTHM, CHARTS AND CHANGES

## TEPONAZTLI

Fat singer in three keys
a continent rolls at your feet.
Gourd gong of the dervishes,
praise your end.
Your tongue slit double,
the mallets stamp your body,
a calked Calliope,
sheer deep in pitch and darkness.
Bone clock of the spirits,
praise your purposes.
Inside, the body,
cut rib upon rib,
howls at the debt the drummer owes.
When the lion climbs
into the skin of a llama,
debtors to ourselves,
we pitch the sound of serpent's feet,
mare's claws, an eagle's brimstone,
and the body screams against
the stamp of a goddess
white as pain.

## Atabaqué

Fat trinity of sisters,
buckle in the Bahia bay,
candomblé;
secret bones and bells
spread in the wine sea.
I am the palm
to blister the tale
                    of your silent origins.
Three heads in one,
blue mirror of a Christian saint,
trapped in your own tarikh,
I name each one batá, ilú,
                    cuica, urucungo.
I name each one: tambor-de-jongo,
                    agogô, adjá.
Secretly, you take the print
                            of heaven's foot
from my body,
disguise me in the cloth
my mother weaves at night.
I go out by day,
anxious to redeem the crocodile
who lurks in the heart of Rio,
but I am captive
                            up the coast.
A fisherman without a net,
I take only stone.
My grain turns to weed.    Birds die in flight.
The cougar chokes. Bananas turn black on the vine.
So I carry the quilombo on my back,
with the wine jugs, caged birds, fridges
                            and imperial beds.
Now in a fufu bowl,
in hen's milk, in tiger grain,

I set your eyes as spies.
Sisters, deep in the carved ribs
I hear your voices begin to call
the ones who would still bear your names,
the gods who would understand
the lace of your labor, the offense
of being only your own.

## BANDOLA

*G*

Tipsy breather,
breathing
is a sense
unsolved.
Five of you,
begad,
sharp as
a G bead string.
Teams of musketeers
muscling for a place
on the board.
Cat gut
is your
only voice.
Some steel you,
gut beneath
the wind.
Quinto requinto.
A wine sound.
Chairman of the board.
Gaffer,
this is the gaff
to gaff the gaffer.
Tune your G.

*d*

Dolorosa,
what is heaven
but the breath
of that string
taken from the gaffer's
winding sheet?

Dolorosa,
ecstasy is the deepest
sound of mourning.
This key
is the angel's coffin;
this chord
is the trumpet's
announcement
of its velvet absence.
Dolorosa,
what is the sin in pity,
the heartbreak
when a child's voice
scans the night?
Trio of clarity,
in the darkness of your pitch,
I hear my absent voice
absent itself from angels
and the air they ride
to flesh the bones that here
my doves will dance upon.

*a*

Má lover of god
Má loved by god
Má of the sun
Má of the river
Má of the timber
Má of the wood
Má of the grief
Má Teodora
What source
is in your circle?
Why do you dance
with the *palo codal*?
What itch constrains

your orisha limp?
Who is the simp
to arrange your fall?
Má Má Teodora
fifteen sinners
guide you through the berries
of your own exultation.
Fifteen lines and a stick
make a whip
to remind you of the grave.
Fifteen stones and a star
lift you to a cloud
beyond my reach.
Má loved by god
you ride your flesh so surely
the gods within the flat drums
keep a tap
upon the earth.

*e'*

There is a harmony
the earth elects.
This boy,
with a witch's staff,
will search it out.
Doctor of the ditching rod,
the groom of charges,
disciple of monkey skulls
—the blood and bearded eye—
he paddles, bootless,
over the hidden water.
Under his light baton,
the ewes are combed,
the ram runs down his bass,
the froth of it
now dry in the clay.

Agnus dei.
What fine motets
these shepherds sing,
remembering our own
                                        and 'civilized
                                                lady.'

*b′*

High bells and xylophones,
marimbas, a courteous guitar,
New England winter in a choir
of fifteen, dressed in Quechua shawls.

What sun is breaking on the pines?

This choir's jungle teeth
sparkle in the fountain.
I bang the drum and pay the toll.
My lover will wake tonight
at the height of a cold Thanksgiving,
and rise from her bed
to take the hidden rose from her hair.
So will the strings lament
                                        her indifference,
her body out of tune
with the balustrade's desire,
the light of a crafty night
setting on a pain so distant
darkness is our joy.
I choose the miracle
                                    of the whale's voice,
the map of an ocean
deep enough to be green,
unplumbed
except for the shell of your voice,
unmarked

except for the wreath of your hair.
I bring my love on these silver spires,
fifteen lucid lines to the cathedral
of your ecstasy.
This is the difficult round,
'a linked sweetness long drawn out,'
the design of the body's expectation,
the ear's vision.

## Huehuetl

Upright,
tight,
caressed for any tone of voice,
jaguar tree,
the legends deepen
in your bowels.
Silent now,
you keep my rage,
my purple primness,
blood red crown,
the journeys set at sea's edge
into the forest's shadows.
I ride a horse, under mail,
into the plume's sunset;
I hear the cough of the prince,
dying in his garden.
Dead in my own garden,
courtier of my shame,
I am two souls in one,
like you a hollow log,
a jaguar skin,
                    fleeced of justice.
I stand still,
in whatever moon appears,
wounded by my own betrayal.
Night of the moons,
you will not run
from the voice
these creole hands
will beat from me.
Under the wing of the jaguar tree,
I rise upright, tight,
caressing my own power.

## Areito

This is my mitote,
batoco,
areito,
my bareitote.
This is my bareitote,
areito, batoco,
my a-ba-mitote.

Corre, corrido, navideño.

Friday the thirteenth
and snow in the birch.
Love's days all begin
with that kind of coldness.
We had come down
to the fog and the bite of the sea,
another of love's soft nibbles
                                        on the skin.
The axe had chipped in the trees.
High up, the squabble of birds
through the evergreens
became the painful sound of palms.

And the woman sang:
*I've got love all around me*
*My own treasure's found me*
*My savior*
*is a boy in bloom.*

So you guess that I wrestled
the shadows of my cabin at night.
My wife, in her corner,
tumbled over the milk in her sleep.

We had arrived
with more than a small purchase,
a small reparation,
                                   to make.
Was it only the axe wronged in the trees?
My skin is the repository
of the sun's needles.
Why had I chosen the cold?

And the woman sang:
*Flesh of my flesh, I nurse your dreams*
*I nurse your screams*
*I am*
*your mother.*

Mystic rose of the heart,
how could three of us
be imprisoned there?
And how could we come
from the dark wood into the light
yet still hear the moonlit canticles
prey in the water,
still pray in another tongue
for sunlight on our nets?
Three of us to nurse the night,
and three of us for saving.
Santos and serpents,
tangled in the streams of our bodies,
dance in the blue of our altar lights.

*Dolor, dolori, passa*
*A strength in a weary land*
*A shelter in the time of a storm.*

I had lived alone with the woman,
sunlight, a son, fish, the fallen apples,

the holy deer that would kneel to our knife,
all the provisions of prayer,
to find myself unmarried,
my woman drunk with God,
nurse of a savior's screams.
Then out of the woods,
I turned to the woods,
to the toothless nurse of my own dreams.
By the light of the thirteenth moon,
I began to search for my own light.

*Wood of the woods*
*Bird of the woods*
*Woman you were created by God.*

Necromancer of the hummingbird,
I bring you this bird's body
and the thirteen rings of my love's chains.
I bring you the secret whispers
of my wife's sleep,
the tangled passions of the forest,
the thorn I would return
                                        to another heart.

*Bird of the woods, fly into her heart.*

Teach me how to stalk her sleep
and the bible of her loves.
Teach me the darkness of thirteen moons,
how to contend with a God.
Bathe me in love's coldness.
Woman of the woods.

*Dolor, dolori, passa.*

I lie down in the sand
to hear my batoco,
my mitote,
my areito,
end.

## Joropo

Finger this my cactus, come now,
won't you buy now? Take now. Oh, how
thick can this rope of your heart be?
Sausage of my sausage, you see
it cut fat clean before your eyes.
*Canta, comal*, my eyes are wise.
*Todo pica*. Cactus? No sin
in the *piña* rings, thin as thin,
delicate haloes on your thumb.
Oh, my friend, I am not so dumb
to think you came this way by chance.
*Piña? Pulque?* Tea? Shall we dance?

## Lundú

Moonlight, if I sleep on this bank
and lay my head against your kiss,
I recognize the river's sound.
Timeless me, all day I raise
my knife against the sugar cane,
sugar brute who takes my days for pay.
Sun glow in spring is crystal clean.
Sun glow north, sun glow south,
sun glow summer, sun glow fall.
The fall of sweetness weighs me.
Aribú of the sweetest god,
will this or what winter
be the longest sleep?
I serenade his green fingers,
his water's magic, his boot in the earth,
the way he pulls the green crowns to light.
Aribú of the grainy god,
will this or what fall
be the desolation of our mother?
I serenade the return of even light
to her wrinkled face.
Moonlight, now I lie on the crown
of my own desire,
hutched
in the fall of the god,
the fall of the cane,
the fall of my own night.

## Son

titocotí    tocotí    tocotí

Blue bird, heron light,
you own the river bank.
I am only your turquoise shield,
the temple's decorative stone,
and so I serve.
And if I take my fee
in great jades and wide quetzal feathers,
I serve.

titocotí    tocotí    tocotí

You sit on a moss mat,
the river's seat.
Your eye goes from deep to deep.
The sun reflects the light above,
the light reflects your love.

tocotí

Myself deep in the water,
I see the mother take her breast
from the baby's mouth.
I see the father walk his fields alone.
I see the child, made fit for war,
turn to slash himself.

Orphans of the earth,
owl-eyed for evil,
we serve ourselves
and know it is no service.
Hunched on the tip of the rain,
we clamor foot-long for the earth.

Fetish-eyed in love,
we know the trick of leaving.
Woman, you are another's pleasure.
You will be abandoned. You will go away.

¡Día de llanto, día de lágrimas!

My tongue is coral,
my lips are emerald.
Feather flame, lucid *guacamaya*,
accept the service of your humble shield.
I write beside your emblem
my father's name,
my mother's name,
your name and mine.
Temple stone, the god endures
such service as you give.
So has the book been written.
So has your heart become perfect.

## Tamborito

Four things, I know,
will never change.
I lie forever in the bed
of my cross,
north wind, south wind,
east rain, west rain.
The walls become my cross.
Tlequilitl.
I huddle the fire between my legs,
and light this room.
I am solid.
I am the measure of the house.
I sleep with my grainy eyes
plucking the shadows from the room.

*A hummingbird, a forest flower*
*brought me to this house.*
*My bones crushed in a pilon,*
*I took my lover.*

Comalli.
Clay, I lay
myself flat,
and, under my mother's touch,
I learn to serve.
When I am no longer in use,
I stand dejected
near the burnt-out fire
I danced upon.

*A hummingbird, a forest flower*
*brought me to this house.*
*My bones crushed in a pilon,*
*I took my lover.*

Metlapilli.
Blunt image of the love man's roller pin,
I roll the juices from the gods' first fruits.
A hammer, I am forever raised
above the heart of this house.

*A hummingbird, a forest flower*
*brought me to this house.*
*My bones crushed in a pilon,*
*I took my lover.*

Now I am a mambo.
My açon croaks.
Now I am a mambo,
married to beads and snake's bones.

I call my Maîtresse
Erzulie Fréda Dahomin,
Venus of Dahomey,
Bride of the Loas.
I pierce her heart,
Lady of the Seven Sorrows.
I stand to the music
of my great, grate,
grateful, grating heart,
perfect rhythm of a heart
that never changes.

# Vela

. . . cawMacaw of the rain forest.
Marigolds and bright banana leaves
light the road,
and yet the darkness closes in.
Too late,
I light your death with candles.
My feet in sandals,
I am a pilgrim
where the pilgrims wind
and beat their sorrows
at a Virgin's hem.
Tambora call.
The flutes call.
The scented candles call.
I call you,
            Langston,
to a forest of beads,
choir of a Virgin's call for you.
Ave,
sing,
southern dangers ride
even the Virgin's wing.
María,
here,
a dead man floats
until you claim him.
I cannot claim
your sorrows for my friend.
Pilgrims with pity for themselves
follow me
with bleached skulls
and thorn-wrapped hearts,
follow me
with save us for our pity.

Can they remember
that you gave me fruit
from these forests, corn from these hills?
The gift redeems.
The gift is a debt of adoration,
an invitation to a shrine,
the blind path of the pure
who honor the light
the grave keeps.
Your grave keeps me restless.
Riding on a bed of marigolds,
I rub the glass before your saint,
massage my forehead with the bloom,
which may contain your grace.

## VILLANCICO

*Love in a body, love in this your sign.*
*I raise four moons to polish your love's shine.*
*I raise four stars to see you as you stand.*
*You take me, in debt now to your own hand.*

You take your white dress from the waves. No stain
appears upon the water where your train
curls lacy from a ram's horn, hugger bane
of eight young brides. Could I myself now chain
you to a monster rock to take the rain
of my love, horned, I hear the bell and plain
chant far out of time. My love is the line
you ride from the deep, and I ride the brine.

*Love in a body, love in this your sign.*
*I raise four moons to polish your love's shine.*
*I raise four stars to see you as you stand.*
*You take me, in debt now to your own hand.*

My antelope, my horse, there is no rein,
ram's horn, bull's bell or god's eye to constrain
you in the fields of love; there is no sane
man who would touch your knees, or hope to gain
the secret of your clan hunger, the skein
of your bones, wave of your heart's deepest vein.
Your love sits on my heart, a heavy wine
I give my untouched body at your shrine.

*Love in a body, love in this your sign.*
*I raise four moons to polish your love's shine.*
*I raise four stars to see you as you stand.*
*You take me, in debt now to your own hand.*

Faithful one, you come, wind before the rain.
Bean-bred, corn-fed, lady of the bead chain,

you hold an axe above your own domain,
where no ram dare plough, seed or shake his mane.
In the thorough-bass of your river plane,
I hear your name assault a priest, a brain
unfit to take a wife's caress, the whine
of the child's voice, hidden in this design.

*Love in a body, love in this your sign.*
*I raise four moons to polish your love's shine.*
*I raise four stars to see you as you stand.*
*You take me, in debt now to your own hand.*

There is pity in your name; in the reign
of your compassion, crown of love, you strain
to harvest pity on a bed of grain.
Widow of death, bride of change, you remain
the copy of the thorny heart, the vein
split free and open by another's pain.
Love, not your own, comes. You cannot decline
your body's burden, the redeeming sign.

*Love in a body, love in this your sign.*
*I raise four moons to polish your love's shine.*
*I raise four stars to see you as you stand.*
*You take me, in debt now to your own hand.*

So where my eyes have seen four moons constrain
these four stars to orbit and to ordain
a pythoness, a body yields, humane,
to the eyes' grasp, to the touch of plain
light. From orbit to orbit I retain
now all the distance of your body, drain
what light alone that it, my anodyne,
leaves, what touch it gives from your spirit's spine.

## Pututu

What would you trade
for the sound of spring
                              in gazelle eyes,
for the sound of night in lilies,
of fire in the plantain,
of rain in a woman's bones?
What would you give
to hear the dove domed by the wind,
the doe caressed by the darkest
                              leaves of the forest?
I come from the river
under the mountain's claw,
and bring my daemon shells,
my god's penny change,
to tune your ears again.
Erect in the river's light,
I have my lance and flags at hand,
my body cased in the colors
of the lives that rise
in the blood of my horn.
I would rule you in the ooze
of my shell, or take you in
with the watery breath
that returns my song to my spine.
Pututu is the sound of your soul's ears
returning to my light.

## Maracas in Merengue

Nothing suave,
a thief of beads,
snake bones
tickle your tum
and oil your neck.
I take your gaudy skin in hand.
I clutch your throat.
I rattle your eyes.
I free your fangs,
the cackle of your prophecies,
the high pitch of my wounds.
I find you everywhere.
Chucho, guache, carángano,
you are a devil's dance,
or the piper forty days from the cross,
the lover's kick,
or the dead man's trace,
the first light in the east.
Witness of the lilies' rising,
consort of the evergreen,
you are the keeper of my wife's
ringed eyes,
the anchoritic daemon
of my own dark forest.
The poor man cooks his hatred
in your bowels.
The mother, with a drunken son
at sea, snaps your jaws
around the silence of her heart.
You use us all.
We are all used up.
One day beyond the dimming
of the lights,
you will goad the dust to rise,
the air to charge the earth
with our absence.

## Bambuco

Face to face,
in faith,
my face,
a lyric mask,
becomes you.
I am at your grill again.
Your ribbon laces my ox
to your door.
Invite me, woman,
to the music of your middle.
I go one foot before the other,
leap back,
begin again from heel to toe.
You mirror my hesitation.
My nerve is in your back.
One foot before the other.
Leap back.
I pinch your waist,
and guide you through
the labyrinths of love's
first petals.
I take your straight body
through the maze of my arms.
I fold my arms,
and touch the swords of yours.
I pass,
unbalanced by your face.
I court your kisses
while your body fades.
My life
is the middle of this dance.
My heart unfolds
to accept this cross,
the stone of our customary light.
Fire-ladened, river-burdened,
a bird indeed,

a blue knit shawl of moonlight,
you chase yourself before me,
you measure my soul's intent,
my clan craft,
the weight of my memory,
the distance of my father's fire.
I spread this shrunken white veil,
and call your step across the river.
I kneel,
and hear your familiar voice
call me home.

# LOGBOOK OF JUDGMENTS

## What Is Good

Out of the water call
my luminous breath,
into the bird, intending serpent, red,
who shakes himself, white,
out of that forest body, black.

Red gourd head spirit of the bush,
your breath is speech;
your speech is ordinary, pure.
I take you from the blue
glass of my sacred windows,
I ring you cold upon my father's weights.

I would cook and save you
in my body's house alone, light
you in the useless prism of my own desires.
I hold you in the yellow
parchment of my soul's hand.
Once I took your body for the shape
of all I walked upon, your god's voice
for the sound of all my light.
But now I count my sins against
the ordinary syntax of my days.

Bird of the hard wood,
I would transcend the dog
and fox of my father's prayers,

the corn, the monkey, lion and the seed
cut crudely by the cross in gold,
the black figures of a Christian death.

Bird, so you would change,
and flutter in my mother's eyes.
And in my mother's eyes
still bodies have rhythms of their own.
The light of dead hearts, my governors,
leads my body to a stillness.
I speak of stillness, and you see
I still grip your rhythm to my body.

Rhythm of my shade, an elephant skin.
Rhythm of my hat, the llama's hair.
Rhythm of my coat, the cactus' beard.
Rhythm of my trousers, silkworm web.
Rhythm of my shoes, pig hips.
Rhythm of my seat, the heart of a tree.
Rhythm of my hands in the beads.
Rhythm of my hands in the cleansing water,
of my eye in the perfect form of stillness,
the perfect light of my mother's ecstasy.

Composed, I am saved
by my mother's reason,
my neighbors' needs,
my will to go beyond the stillness
of my gods' dreams.
Luminous breath,
teach me compassion for this
my complex body.

## What Is True

I argue my woman into compassion.
Light upon light, through darkness,
she gives me what is true.
Radiant light is in the river bed,
morning's collocation,
the linchpin of the hours' flow.
The source of illumination
is in the jaw of the willow,
clinching the earth, the juice
that inches from the broken cactus ear.
A lily dead upon the water veils the altar.
A star ascending reaches its
own domain, its own rest.
But here we balance in the moon fall,
and chart the absence in a curve,
upon a clock,
the solitary body where the world ends.
Composed,
we name the caves from which we rise.
Profane and strange, our dead arrive
with linen and scented candles,
salt beer, sweet wine,
tapered beads, a bright
wood for the altar.
It seems that nothing in this light
will fade or be used up.
And so I take their meanings
from my woman's sign,
their changes from her absence.
I take her passion for my head,
her craft into my heart.
Love measures me.
Love pays me out.

Love gives me my domain.
My radiance is a red bead,
a white feather on a bow,
balanced on my grave.

## What Is Beautiful

Now I invest the world
with a song of your flesh,
song of your bones, your blood, your heart.
I pitch all dark things still
to the scale of my voice.
I name what I distinguish.
I discern what rises without a name.
Here, there is no form untuned by eye, or voice;
there is no body waiting for its metaphor.
My canon gathers all the turnings
of your light, all the offices
and arguments of your soul's intent.
Your body has a province in my two worlds,
begins its own exchange in my eye.
So as my music is exampled only
in the movement, so is your body simplified,
made absolute and able to bear
the god's chill piping in your bones,
his red eye scanning your skin.
But I do not shape you two-in-one,
or call you from the darkness,
a scruffy thing, enhanced and visible
only when the light leaves you.
I turn you to the tuning fork of solid
walls, my rolled corn, my tiled squares,
the rose windows of my altars.
I turn your ear, now transformed,
to the imperfection of sacred things,
your body's distant vibrations.
And so each element of my song moves,
and my voice takes back its absence,
my eye searches a new light, another exchange.
This is the gift of being transformed,
the emptiness that calls compassion down.

I pitch my eye to my uneven form,
my voice to the depths of your grace.
I reason with the sound and movement
of your body to the vision
                    that my body bears.

## Meta-A and the A of Absolutes

I write my God in blue.
I run my gods upstream on flimsy rafts.
I bathe my goddesses in foam, in moonlight.
I take my reasons from my mother's snuff breath,
or from an old woman, sitting with a lemonade,
at twilight, on the desert's steps.
Brown by day and black by night,
my God has wings that open to no reason.
He scutters from the touch of old men's eyes,
scutters from the smell of wisdom, an orb
of light leaping from a fire.
Press him he bleeds.
When you take your hand to sacred water,
there is no sign of any wound.
And so I call him supreme, great artist,
judge of time, scholar of all living event,
the possible prophet of the possible event.
Blind men, on bourbon, with guitars,
blind men with their scars dulled by kola,
blind men seeking the shelter of a raindrop,
blind men in corn, blind men in steel,
reason by their lights that our tongues
are free, our tongues will redeem us.
Speech is the fact, and the fact is true.
What is moves, and what is moving is.
We cling to these contradictions.
We know we will become our contradictions,
our complex body's own desire.
Yet speech is not the limit of our vision.
The ear entices itself with any sound.
The skin will caress whatever tone
or temperament that rises or descends.
The bones will set themselves to a dance.
The blood will argue with a bird in flight.

The heart will scale the dew from an old chalice,
brush and thrill to an old bone.
And yet there is no sign to arrest us
                                        from the possible.
We remain at rest there, in transit
from our knowing to our knowledge.
So I would set a limit where I meet my logic.
I would clamber from my own cave
into the curve of sign, an alphabet
of transformation, the clan's cloak of reason.
I am good when I am in motion,
when I think of myself at rest
in the knowledge of my moving,
when I have the vision of my mother at rest,
in moonlight, her lap the cradle of my father's head.
I am good when I trade my shells,
and walk from boundary to boundary,
unarmed and unafraid of another's speech.
I am good when I learn the world
through the touch of my present body.
I am good when I take the cove of a cub
                                                into my care.
I am good when I hear the changes in my body
echo all my changes down the years,
when what I know indeed is what I would
                                                  know in deed.
I am good when I know the darkness of all light,
and accept the darkness, not as sign, but as my body.
This is the A of absolutes,
the logbook of judgments,
the good sign.

# FROM
# *THE DOUBLE INVENTION OF KOMO*
# (1980)

# THE ABSTRACT OF KNOWLEDGE / THE FIRST TEST

I shall be the last to come into the word
and into the power of the word;
by these I will address the god and command all things.
And yet abstraction bears me down.
Brother, you have given me
    the instruments' cloth
        and the altars' dance,
the figure in the field,
    your mother body
        and my name's inclination.
I have the mask's teeth in my flesh.
I pitch my soul's desire in the jackal's
black knowledge, twin head of copper's light.
The sound of your voice is the first tone
in the cycle of redemption,
            love's prefiguration.
I grow by an intimation of a first act,
by the clear presence of a fixed grave.
I urge my spirit through desire's cure.
I buckle into virtue's space.
Still, I am divested of my love's
endurable space; the god must be
divested of my body's space.

What is the question?

Who will hurry into this absence
to instruct a spirit uneasy
        in its double knowledge?

And so I struggle with the locus of desire
and with my own intervention.

Am I the mouth of the beast,
the child of abasement,
father of the little double?
Am I doubled in every presence,
in every grave in the wood,
prefigured in every public act?
Does the light gather the *doṅu* bird's wings
          in the same,
                    peristaltic motion?
Will the river always return the same shells,
the same bones, the same serpent rhythm?

What is the question?

What prefiguration empties the world of desire?
Where is the figure to lift me into love?

An idiot initiate is evil's shaft of light.
If you go from the certainty of oneness
into solitude and return,
I must divest you of your double
and twin you in love's seclusion.
My instruments toll you into limbo;
the altars know the music of your name.
You arrive by being absent.
The light must be brought where the body lies.
And, where the body, in its wisdom, rises,
the head is time's scalpel and suture.
The body is a schema of desire;
the head, the seat of the act.
You understand that all things beg
to be undone and returned to the first act.
Even the master comes to the wood,
even he sits in the dark, under the telling,
to listen for the first term,
the tree leaves' first trembling,
the star's bellow in the pool.

I continue.

A double vision wants a double state.
A double heart urges the black band to appear.
This is my hand on the tunic.
Your hand shuttles back the black band's absence.
We invest the cloth with nothing,
no thread to bridge us from the gold wood home.
We must speak of heaven,
or the ordinal of one, light's preference
for the habitation of the appointed.
We must specify the double nature of purity,
and the equipoise of space on the point of desire.
Now, when the master prepares his boat
and assumes love's service,
light erects his cause and generation.

I continue.

Conception's conceiver.
Nothing names a rhythm,
taking itself for a cause,
doctor of its own root and effort,
instance of its own birth.
Will the god sit,
becalmed in his boat,
to be embraced by one
who will not name him?
I insist that I hold
designation's deepest vibration
in my body. I know myself,
by grace,
to be the principle of all things.
Out of every hidden emblem,
I extol the act I cannot name.

I must tell you of the seven phases
of my seven forms.

Here, I have the design
of all disengaged things,
my acts and heavens,
earths, plants, and beasts, my person.
I profess my master's praise
and my own faith,
my first contesting of my faith.
I order your allegiance, now,
to the signs' immaculate
appearance, a sortie
into divinity's turbulence;
to the irruption of desire's cocoon,
and its emerging;
to the spirit's turning and return
to the master's voice;
to the token of divine serenity;
to love's conception, birth,
and revelation.
I would have you grow in the signs' unfolding.
I would discover you in the resurrection of sacred things.

I am arguing with the movement of desire.
I have great signs to unhouse my twin,
to perfect my singularity.
I turn
twelve ways.
I appear
and disappear.
I have great signs to disclose
one word,
one expression,
one member of a phrase.
The signs assure my birth
and penetration,
and assure my good
and covenant with you.
These emblems set me down before the stars,

turned stone in the yellow dust.<br>
I must be advised by darkness,<br>
        by an exploratory smith,<br>
            who hammers copper's light<br>
                                            from earth,<br>
to forge it in secret.<br>
            My own darkness<br>
            gives me<br>
            back<br>
            to Yuri and Dya,<br>
to the burnished darkness<br>
        of my blind saint.<br>
I take this road again<br>
to articulate my discontent<br>
with what is given.<br>
                                  I have learned<br>
that there is a blessing<br>
in my body's disrupted blood.<br>
                                  I contend<br>
that I will not be self-slain,<br>
            borne on heaven's tree<br>
            to engage<br>
                        my own knowledge.

            I ask,<br>
            then,<br>
            how I will come<br>
into possession of my body,<br>
            how I will<br>
circle<br>
        the stone of my desire<br>
        and face you on love's edge.<br>
I must construct a reason<br>
for light's withdrawal;<br>
                                        I must<br>
combat destruction's caravan<br>
and the slave heart bred

by the pool's intentional retreat.
This,
        my celibate courage,
tokens the mask's
                            abandonment.

If I were the light's sacred buffoon,
I could read this meaning and mount
my own awakening;
I could carry a great saber
        on the rib
                of a palm leaf,
and call it my knife
        to provoke
                my own descent.
But the anvil awakens me:
        Mandé,
        Keita,
        Asante,
my Bandiagara kin.
I claim my complex body.
I proclaim
the lot of the great old man
is a progress toward death,
the unknown,
the nothing,
the creator.

Who goes first?
The black band on the tunic
answers, God; the sign, no one.
If the word speaks itself,
there will be nothing,
no measure, no balance,
no temper, no pure body
lying in state,
no sound attending
its own procession.

I circle and face myself.
I cannot ask who goes first.

What is the question?

What is the first act?

It would be easy to sketch
a cape and crown,
an encompassing arm,
a figure trunked up
on air and golden light,
boneless, fleet,
and contentious.
Love's office would be
inhabited;
desire's embryo
would edge from its shell.

I turn.
I continue.

I define the seed
as a calling.
In this appointment,
I find I have no delegate,
no eye to examine
the seed's vocation.
I cannot say
I enter with God,
at the music's first insistence,
or that I am in the seed's whine,
in its authoritative spiral
into its bowels.
Inside itself,
the seed hears
its ache of being,
its reason to twist its voice

into understanding.
The seed of my being
does not exist,
except in the act
of taking notice.
Before the body,
there is an act;
before the act,
there is desire.
The ear of an unfigured head
begins the descent.
I shape the head an absent
two-in-one, an auditory
acquaintance
with designation's dance.
This failing comforts me.
Under the gold light of the primal wood,
I accept the chastity of all things.

You see I have the faculty
of being absent.
That is the lesson I take
from the first light
and from the unseizable god
whose trembling bells him
out of the anvil to my side.
Father—I call you—
spirit of the apprehension
of absence, the precedent
refusal.
In our blindness,
we entreat the seed's song.

We must have a language
to annotate the seed's ascent.
There is a message
in the seed's turning,

a disposition to be heard,
to sit in every initiate's scale,
inviolable,
sovereign of its voice
and understanding.
This, when the soul taps its cup
to be filled with its own sacrament,
you must understand.
There is a message in the failure
to transpose what can be spoken.
The seed's roll and yaw define
what can be spoken.
I take my cloud body to the pool
to bathe in light.

What is the question?

I turn.
I continue.
I address myself.

Initiate,
under the ladder,
two spirits stand.
Sómá has no twin.
He loves his lamb's role
and the armor he puts on
in the altars' service.
You find him in worship's constant eye.
His name, life's form, reveals his task.
The other is your body
into this body,
a manifest of your soul's intent.
By their sanctity and sacrifice,
these go first,
nearest to God,
auditors of the seed's voice.

Nothing can precede a death
they do not give you.
There is no salvation,
without their example.
You must know they teach
the art of giving up,
the initiate's crawl into love's circle.
If, in the deepest foundation,
you give voice to their names,
they will protect you from the questioning
of love's first act.
Celibate Sómá defines you.
You take his chaste and sober
shadow into charity.
Zando pulls you from your cave into Sómá's art,
into the prophecy of death and return.
You sleep and awake in the sleeper's design.
The sleeper sustains you.
The dream binds you in love's intent.
You bear resurrection's cure
in your spirit's polar
modulation,
in the way a mother takes
a child's first computations
into her care,
and in the exact crib
of the river's course,
the sun's catenary elation,
the plow's trenching,
the weaver's needle in the cloth,
the mariner's silver plumb line in the water,
the mason's plinth,
in the altars' bull-bell and whine,
in the risk of your heart's
executive speculation.
You endure in the exact
apprehension

of what you do not possess.
Thief-heart,
you prepare for grace
and the heart's redemptive
brocade, the woman,
subject of her twin tribulation,
who unveils the flower of the kapok tree,
the soul's solstice, engraved on calabash,
dabbed in the blood of the dispossessed.
Mousso Koroni,
keeper of the children of shame,
harbinger of my body's first loss,
your galleon conjuration galls me.
I now traverse love's dispersal
through your body,
here,
in an exile's scriptorium.
Love itself allows your opposition.
Say that love permits me
to publish my own decline,
to here, where I am pitched up,
waterless, a water spirit compelled
toward a denser wood.
Now, may your necessary injury
guide me to what is true.
What is true is the incision.
What is true is the desire for the incision,
and the signs' flaming in the wound.

I am now your delegate.
I give you order and determination,
and your soul's syntax,
extracted from God's speech.

I continue.
I speak.

(Rome)
*"He who puts on wisdom, puts on grief;*
*and a heart that understands cuts*
*like rust in the bones."*
*—Augustine*

"It is yearning that makes the heart deep."
Put on your traveling shoes.
Walk, out of the pool,
beside the Great Fish,
sandals on my feet
to keep the earth away.
Only the righteous shall enter.
In the holy water of your heart,
lies a shut-in garden,
a sealed fountain, a well-spring
of living water, a paradise
bearing the fruit of apples.
Strap holiness and renunciation
to your feet, buckle the desire
to walk to God to your loins,
walk on the wave of God's mercy,
step down here and sail away
to God in his boat of grace.
Thus, I have you riddling in the temple
—*peregrinus*—never at home in Rome.
Your thirst for water and sails
turns you in a circle.
I hold before your eye
no suffering Christ,
but the Great Word and Wisdom of God.
But, oh, I am old,
and the lions tax me
with my contradictions.
Salvation is now the water
I ride upon,
for my soul,

for this raggèd body,
for this raggèd soul in a raggèd body,
for this pure soul in a pure body.
Can it matter what I say?
I understand only the falling
and the rising up,
under every inconceivable power.
This, as I am old, my heart tells me.
And so I take the tattered sail
of my body, under the tattered
sail of a Rome-bound boat,
in a fortunate wind,
away from my mother.
Water had bound me.

> "I carried about me a cut and bleeding soul,
> that could not bear to be carried by me,
> and where I could put it, I could not discover.
> Not in pleasant groves, not in games and singing,
> nor in the fragrant corners of a garden. . . .
> I remained a haunted spot, which gave me no rest,
> from which I could not escape.
> For where could my heart flee from my heart?
> Where could I escape from myself?
> Where would I not dog my own footsteps?
> —I left my hometown."

And left the most unfathomable
of all involvements,
        and the mother.
And entered the double sorrow of death,
agèd tolerance and a late patience.
And entered Ambrose's other world,
to disfigure the simple opposition
of light and the dark,
to return to the shadows
        on God's face.
No one loves what he cannot,
in understanding, make his own.

This is the dance of the changeless
and the changing,
the spirit's intensity
for the world's endurance.
Knowledge is motion in twilight,
a state of falling into sight;
one by one,
the spirit's eyes touch and grow.
*Peregrinus*, the tense spirit
tenses and returns to its
own understanding.
There is always the going forth
and the returning;
there is always the act,
the slow fusion of being.
All things,
by the strength of being joined,
will continue;
the sin is to turn away;
ignorance is inattention
to the voice, which feeds you.

> "Let them deal harshly with you,
> who do not know with what effort
> truth is found and with what
> difficulty errors are avoided . . .
> who do not know with what pain
> the inner eye of a man is healed,
> that he may glimpse his Sun."

The act grows from delight,
prepared by the hidden,
quivering arrow of a god's hand.
The act is in the longing for God's hand,
or your own hand, in the act.

> "Grant me to wind round and round
> in my present memory the spirals
> of my errors . . ."

and of my longing.
This Easter Eve of double death
                    and double resurrection,
I join the competent ones
to hear twelve sacramental steps—
the deluge and purified waters,
the passage through a split sea.
Brother blesses the water with the cross,
divides it along the axes of the earth,
along the memory of Paradise.
Christ in the candle enters the water,
sanctifies the water.
Brother takes the Lord in the candle
three times into the tomb.
I step into the fount three times,
to know that I die with the world,
am buried, and rise again.
Brother,
          Thus let us enter together,
          in the path of charity,
          in search of Him . . .
in search of the act,
in search of the meaning of desire.

# AFTERWORD

## By Harold Bloom

I recall purchasing *The Homecoming Singer* in 1971, at the suggestion of John Hollander. The poem that immediately captured me was the penultimate one, the extraordinary "Sketch for an Aesthetic Project," with its exuberant beginning:

> I stomp about these rooms in an old overcoat,
> never warm, but never very anxious
> to trot off to the thickly banked park,
> where the perpetual rain hangs in the trees,
> even on sunny days.

This wry origin indeed flowered into Jay Wright's ongoing aesthetic project, a mythic journey akin to that of Hart Crane, whose invocatory splendor hovers throughout *The Homecoming Singer*. Like Robert Stepto, I hear in Wright something of Robert Hayden, a touch of T. S. Eliot, and a few traces of other makers, but the undoubted precursor is Hart Crane, uncannily present as "Sketch for an Aesthetic Project" nears its conclusion:

> I have made a log for passage,
> out there, where some still live,
> and pluck my bones.
> There are parchments of blood,
> sunk where I cannot walk.
> But when there is silence here,
> I hear a mythic shriek.

If there is an aura of Eliot here, it remains *The Waste Land* as absorbed and countermanded by *The Bridge*. Wright, very early in his poetic career, seems to station himself on Crane's side in the agon with Eliot, choosing mythmaking, with all its hazards, over received faith:

This shriek in the coldness
is like music returning to me,
coming over the illusion of solitude,
swift and mad as I am,
dark in its act,
light
in the way it fills
my pitiless mind.

The directness of this lyricism has never left Wright, but his development after *The Homecoming Singer* has followed his precursor Crane's trajectory, from an initial, heightened, rhetorical art of chant to a conceptually difficult mythmaking. Unlike Crane, Wright is a learned poet, and his interweaving of a dense rhetoricity and an elaborate mythology, African yet as personal as William Blake's, has kept his audience too sparse until now. I do not wish to address myself to the complex matter of Jay Wright's place in Afro-American literary tradition, since I do not qualify as a scholarly critic of that tradition. He seems to me a black poet only as May Swenson is a woman poet or as John Hollander or Irving Feldman is a Jewish poet. The poems of all these establish themselves as powerful utterances *within* the tradition of utterance that is American poetry. Only later do I ponder the relation of Swenson's riddles to Dickinson's, or of Hollander's plangent humor to Moshe Leib Halpern's, or of Wright's rhapsodic liturgies to Hayden's prior transformation of Hart Crane's symbolism in an Afro-American context.

In Wright's powerful book, *Soothsayers and Omens*, the final chant, "The Dead," gives the central statement of his poetics, at least as I comprehend his vision. After admonishing his readers that our learning alone cannot suffice, since "it is not enough / to sip the knowledge / of our failings," the poet chants an intricate rhapsody of the self's return from its own achieved emptiness:

The masks dance
on this small point, and lead

this soul, these souls,
into the rhythm
of the eye stripped of sight,
the hand stripped of touch,
the heart stripped of love,
the body stripped of its own beginning,
into the rhythm
of emptiness and return,
into the self
moving against itself,
into the self
moving into itself,
the word, and the first design.

The *askesis* here is Wright's characteristic apotropaic gesture toward tradition, toward all his traditions. As an immensely learned poet, Wright tries to defend himself against incessant allusiveness by stripping his diction, sometimes to an astonishing sparseness. The same movement in W. S. Merwin has damaged the art of one of our strongest contemporary poets, but Wright's minimalism is fortunately not nearly so prevalent. His most characteristic art returns always to that commodious lyricism I associate with American poetry at its most celebratory, in Whitman, in Stevens, in Crane, in Ashbery. A recent ode, "Desire's Persistence," which may be his strongest poem to date, opens out into a majestic epiphany of what the sage Emerson declared as the American Newness:

WINTER

Under the evergreens,
the grouse have gone under the snow.
Women who follow their fall flight
tell us that, if you listen, you can hear
their dove's voices ridge the air,
a singing that follows us to a bourne
released from its heat sleep.

We have come to an imagined line,
                    celestial,
that binds us to the burr of a sheltered thing
and rings us with a fire that will not dance,
          in a horn that will not sound.
We have learned, like these birds,
to publish our decline,
when over knotted apples and straw-crisp leaves,
the slanted sun welcomes us once again
to the arrested music in the earth's divided embrace.

It is not to be believed, by me, that a verbal art this absolute will continue to suffer neglect. A Pindaric sublimity that allies Hölderlin, Rilke, and Hart Crane with Jay Wright is not now much in fashion, but that mode of high song always returns to us again. As an authentic poet of the Sublime, Wright labors to make us forsake easier pleasures for more difficult pleasures. Wright's reader is taught by him what Hölderlin and Rilke wished us to learn, which is that poetry compels us to answer the fearful triple question: more? equal to? or less than? Self is set against self, or an earlier version of the self against a later one, or culture against culture, or poem against poem. Jay Wright is a permanent American poet because he induces us to enter that agon—with past strength, our own or others'; with the desolations of culture; with the sorrows of history—and because he persuades us also that "it is not enough / to sip the knowledge / of our failings."

PRINCETON SERIES
OF CONTEMPORARY POETS

*Returning Your Call*, by Leonard Nathan
*Sadness And Happiness*, by Robert Pinsky
*Burn Down the Icons*, by Grace Schulman
*Reservations*, by James Richardson
*The Double Witness*, by Ben Belitt
*Night Talk and Other Poems*, by Richard Pevear
*Listeners at the Breathing Place*, by Gary Miranda
*The Power to Change Geography*, by Diana Ó Hehir
*An Explanation of America*, by Robert Pinsky
*Signs and Wonders*, by Carl Dennis
*Walking Four Ways in the Wind*, by John Allman
*Hybrids of Plants and of Ghosts*, by Jorie Graham
*Movable Islands*, by Debora Greger
*Yellow Stars and Ice*, by Susan Stewart
*The Expectations of Light*, by Pattiann Rogers
*A Woman Under the Surface*, by Alicia Ostriker
*Visiting Rites*, by Phyllis Janowitz
*An Apology for Loving the Old Hymns*, by Jordan Smith
*Erosion*, by Jorie Graham
*Grace Period*, by Gary Miranda
*In the Absence of Horses*, by Vicki Hearne
*Whinny Moor Crossing*, by Judith Moffett
*The Late Wisconsin Spring*, by John Koethe
*A Drink at the Mirage*, by Michael J. Rosen
*Blessing*, by Christopher Jane Corkery
*The New World*, by Frederick Turner
*And*, by Debora Greger
*The Tradition*, by A. F. Moritz
*An Alternative to Speech*, by David Lehman
*Before Recollection*, by Ann Lauterbach
*Armenian Papers: Poems 1954–1984*, by Harry Mathews

LIBRARY OF CONGRESS CATALOGING-IN-PUBLICATION DATA

Wright, Jay.
Selected poems of Jay Wright.

(Princeton series of contemporary poets)
I. Stepto, Robert B. II. Title. III. Series.
PS 3573.R5364A6 1987 811'.54 86-43128
ISBN 0-691-06687-6 (alk. paper)
ISBN 0-691-01435-3 (pbk.)